# Contents

*We all die, and although this reality is as much a part of life as birth, thinking about it is not easy. Individually we may plan the treatment we would wish to have towards the end of life, or anticipate the comfort we might find in cultural and religious beliefs, but most of the time we choose to avoid thinking too much about it.*

*Healthcare systems, however, do not have the option of prevarication. Many people already need better care towards the end of life. As well as providing this, healthcare systems must plan now for the care we will all need in the future.*

*(WHO 2004a)*

# Policy in end-of-life care:
# Education, ethics, practice
# and research

## Mary Chiarella

QUAY
BOOKS

A division of MA Healthcare Ltd

Quay Books Division, MA Healthcare Ltd, St Jude's Church, Dulwich Road, London SE24 0PB

British Library Cataloguing-in-Publication Data
A catalogue record is available for this book

© MA Healthcare Limited 2006
ISBN   1 85642 307 7

Printed in the Malta by Gutenberg Press, Gudja Road, Tarxien PLA19

# Foreword

The care of individuals at the end of their lives can be incredibly complex. Clinical staff and those caring for the dying have a multitude of issues to deal with; managing pain and symptom control, attending to the psychological and emotional impact of dying, engaging in collaborative decision making and all while working within relevant ethical and legal frameworks. The majority of dying individuals, their families and professional carers deal with this complexity quietly, carefully and sensitively, however, a number of cases hit the headlines. They do this because the issues are so complex we need to refer to the legal structures in society and seek public views.

In a world where technology means we can keep individuals alive for longer debates about the right to choose, the sanctity of life and the role and responsibility of healthcare staff have never been more important. At the University of Nottingham we have been engaging in research in this area for a number of years. In 2003 we secured funding to set up the Sue Ryder Care Centre for Palliative and End-of-Life Studies and needed a review of international policy relating to palliative and end-of-life care to contextualise the work it would undertake.

Mary Chiarella embarked on this task when she was a visiting professor with us in the School of Nursing. Her brief was to review, analyse and synthesise how policy in this area had developed and what had influenced this development; the legal and ethical frameworks that shape the delivery of palliative and end-of-life care; the concept of personhood and the right of an individual to decide what happens to his or her body; how clinical frameworks drive models of care; international issues in the field; and research and development priorities. This book is the output from her work with us. In it Mary presents a concise and informed review of the issues which we have found useful when determining the direction of research here at Nottingham and which I am sure will also be useful to those working in the field of palliative and end-of-life care whether researcher, clinician or policy maker.

Professor Karen Cox
Professor in Cancer and Palliative care
University of Nottingham
March 2006

# Tables of cases and statutes

## Table of cases

*Airedale NHS Trust v Bland [1993]* 1 All ER 821
*A NHS Trust v D & Ors [2000]* TLR 19/7/2000
*Barber v Superior Court* 147 Cal. App. 3d 1006 (Cal. App. 1983)
*Burke v General Medical Council [2004]* EWHC 1879 (Admin)
*Bush v Schiavo* 885 So. 2d 321 (Fla 2003)
*Bush* 885, So 2d 329 (Fla 2004)
*Cruzan v Director, Missouri Department of Health* 497 US 261 (1990)
*Gardner Re BWV [2003]* VCAT 121
*Glass v United Kingdom (61827/00) [2004]* ECHR 102
*Hudson v Texas Children's Hospital [2005]* Texas App LEXIS 1693
*Malette v Schulman [1990]* 67 DLR (4th) 321
*NHS Trust A v M: NHS Trust B v H [2001]* 1 FCR 406
*Portsmouth NHS Trust v Wyatt [2004]* EWHC 2247 (Fam)
*Pretty v Director of Public Prosecutions and Secretary of State for Home*
    *Department [2001]* EWHC Admin 7882
*Re AK (Medical treatment: consent) [2001]* 1 FLR 129
*Re C (Adult refusal of treatment) [1994]* 1 WWLR 290
*Re Conroy* 89 NJ 321, 398–399 (1985)
*Re J (A Minor) (Wardship: Medical treatment) [1991]* 2 WLR 140
*Re JT (Adult: Refusal of medical treatment) [1998]* 1 FLR 48
*Re L (A child) [2004]* EWHC 2713 (Fam)
*Re MB (Medical treatment) [1997]* 2 FLR 437
*Re MB v a NHS Trust [2002]* EHWC 429 (Fam)
*Re Quinlan* 755 A2A 647 (NJ), 429 US 922 (1976)
*Re Schiavo* 780 So 2d 176, 177 (Fla App 2001)
*Re Schiavo* 8351 So 2d 182 (2003)
*Schloendorff v Society of New York* 105 NE 92, 93 (1914)
*Vacco v Quill* 117 S.Ct.2293, 138 L. Ed. 2d (1997)
*Washington v Glucksberg* 117 S. Ct. 2258, 138 L. Ed. 2d 772 (1997)
*Wyatt v Portsmouth NHS Trust [2005]* EWHC 693 (Fam)

# Tables of statutes

Advance Directives Act (Texas) 1999
Death with Dignity Act (Oregon) 1997
Human Rights Act (UK) 1998
Medical Treatment Act (Vic) 1988
NHS and Community Care Act (UK) 1990
Patient Self-Determination Act (US) 1990
Rights of the Terminally Ill Act (NT) 1995
Termination of Life on Request and Assistance with
    Suicide Act (Netherlands) 2001
Terri's Law 2003 Fla Laws Ch. 418

# CHAPTER 1

# History of the development of end-of-life care

## Introduction

The intent of this book is to provide a review of policy on palliative care and end-of-life care. This chapter provides a background against which to focus the work of the Sue Ryder Care Centre in Palliative and End-of-Life Studies at the University of Nottingham. The terms palliative care and end-of-life care are both used because, although in the past they may have been used interchangeably, today they have discrete meanings. These differences are discussed in detail in *Chapter 4*, but fundamentally palliative care is now considered to be an integral part of the care of anyone with a life-threatening illness and comprises physical, psychological, spiritual and social care. It is expected to be implemented on diagnosis and to continue until death. In contrast, end-of-life care, also known as terminal care or care of the dying would only be introduced in the final stages of a person's life when a diagnosis of dying had been made (Lynn and Adamson, 2003 in WHO, 2004a, p.15).

Policy does not occur in a vacuum. It always exists within some kind of legal framework, be that statutory or common law, and it is also shaped by a range of other influences to a lesser or greater degree. These influences include: the views of key stakeholders; political direction and necessity; current affairs and media; economic and ethical debate; as well as other national and international influences that may be occurring at any given time (Lee *et al*, 2001).

For these reasons, this book will not only focus on past and current policy, but will also explore a number of major issues that recur in the literature. These include: the continuing legal and ethical debates around end-of-life care; considerations around clinical practice from a range of stakeholder perspectives; and the major lobby groups at national and international level who are both leading and influencing the debates. In addition, the book will examine some international trends in policy development, and will conclude by exploring the potential for research, education, future debate and policy development in palliative care and end-of-life care. It is not intended to be an exhaustive review of the literature but it does provide a representative overview of the key issues and arguments and an analysis of past, present and future research, education and policy directions. In particular it focuses on policy and legislation in the UK and USA, although, where relevant, literature from other countries is included.

## Structure of the book

This book is set out in six chapters. *Chapter 1* focuses on the history of the development of end-of-life care as a distinct area of health service provision and maps the political and policy documents that have shaped this progress in the developed world.

*Chapters 2 and 3* overview the legal and ethical frameworks in which palliative care and end-of-life care debates are situated. In addition to identifying the current legal context of palliative care and particularly end-of-life care, they also briefly examine the controversial issues surrounding forgoing life-sustaining treatment, advance directives, proxy decision making, physician-assisted suicide, aid in dying, and euthanasia.

Case law, legislation and policy documents will be drawn on from England, the USA, Australia, Canada and other countries where appropriate. Judgments from other jurisdictions do not exercise any binding precedent on English courts, but are often used in judicial deliberations to elucidate the issues under discussion. *Chapter 2* looks particularly at the notion of personhood in end-of-life care, focusing on the patient's right to decide what happens to his or her body, and particularly the right to refuse treatment. It also examines what happens if patients are unable to refuse treatment due to incapacity, both when their wishes as to treatment are known and when they are not. *Chapter 3* examines therapeutic issues arising in end-of-life care, including the use of opiates and the consequences of refusal of treatment on clinical care.

*Chapter 4* examines the major clinical issues that are currently the subject of debate in the professional literature. The purpose of the chapter is to examine how policy influences clinical practice and which aspects of policy ought to be the focus of attention for clinicians. It does not seek to review the vast array of literature on clinical practice in palliative and end-of-life care. The policy issues that are explored in relation to end-of-life care are: funding; eligibility criteria; location; staffing requirements; clinical frameworks and models of care; and communication models and requirements.

*Chapter 5* takes a snapshot of palliative care and end-of-life care in a selection of other countries that are reported in the literature. In particular it considers the integration of palliative care into mainstream health services and opioid availability in these countries. It does not attempt to undertake a complete examination of palliative care in Europe as this has been comprehensively covered by Henk ten Have and David Clark (2002).

Finally, *Chapter 6* considers the implications of this policy review for future research and policy development, as derived from the literature. The chapter begins with a review of what patients and carers want from end-of-life care, and then looks at policy development and implementation, including educational needs and consumer involvement. Research and evaluation directions are subsequently considered. The chapter seeks to address the elements of future directions for end-of-life care from a perspective of integration.

## History of the development of palliative care and end-of life care as a distinct area of health service provision

### Early stages

Care of the dying has always been a feature of human society. However, it has not always been viewed as a responsibility of healthcare delivery systems. It was only during the twentieth century that people living in developed countries began to imagine, if there were no possibility of a cure for their disease, that there was anywhere to go but home, where they would die in the care of their family and under the ministrations of their local clergyman or spiritual carer (Kellehear, 2001; MacLeod, 2002). In developing countries today, this is often still the case. Many people throughout the world are dying without adequate pain control, as only 48% of countries reported having morphine available even in specialist cancer treatment hospitals (WHO, 2003a). While today the majority of people in developed countries still wish to die at home, they hope to do so in a supportive atmosphere that ensures good pain and symptom control (WHO, 2004a).

The early work relating to care of the dying is often traced back to the Middle Ages. Religious orders established hospices that offered shelter to pilgrims on their way to visit shrines, many in the hope of cures for incurable illnesses, and many of whom therefore died in the hospices during their journey. This form of care for the dying (particularly the dying poor) continued through the religious orders into the nineteenth century. In the early twentieth century the Irish Sisters of Charity opened St Joseph's Hospice in London and St Luke's Hospice and the Hospice of God were also opened to serve the destitute dying in the early twentieth century. From 1957 to 1967 Cicely Saunders worked at St Joseph's Hospice and became particularly interested in the management of pain in the dying (Hospice Education Institute, undated). She established St Christopher's Hospice in 1967 (Saunders, 1985) and was influential in establishing the hospice movement at Yale following a visit in 1963 (National Hospice and Palliative Care Organization, undated).

Hospices were developing in Communist Poland in the mid 1970s (Luczak *et al*, 2002) and in Russia the first hospice was founded in 1990 (Wright,

2003). In the USA the work of Elizabeth Kübler-Ross sparked widespread professional and public interest in death and care of the dying throughout the 1970s (Kübler-Ross, 1993). As a result of such pioneering work hospices as we now know them were established which provided palliative care mainly, but not exclusively, to people dying from cancer. Funding of palliative and end-of-life care will be discussed in *Chapter 4*.

### Early policy development

Much of the policy work in the 1970s and 1980s related to the care of cancer patients and the management of cancer pain. In particular, there was concern among international bodies to ensure that patients suffering from pain had access to opioid analgesics. The United Nations had adopted the Single Convention on Narcotic Drugs (the Convention) in 1961 (amended in 1972), whose role it was to regulate all aspects of narcotic drugs for medical use. The purpose of the Convention was and is to combat illicit drug trafficking, but it did not wish to limit the use of narcotics for legitimate medical purposes such as pain management. The Convention has always sought to achieve balance between the control of illicit drug use and ensuring the availability of opioids to treat pain and provide relief for medical conditions (Dahl, 2002).

Notwithstanding the intent of the Convention, it is clear from the policy history that there were many countries that erred (and still err) strongly on the side of caution in making opioids available to those requiring palliative and end-of-life care. The management of pain, and particularly cancer pain, was such a significant issue that in 1982 the World Health Organisation (WHO) convened a meeting of pain management experts in Milan to develop draft guidelines on the management of cancer pain. In 1984 in Geneva a further WHO meeting was held on the comprehensive management of cancer pain and this resulted in the 1986 WHO publication *Cancer Pain Relief*, which also included the amended 1982 draft guidelines. Over 160 000 copies of the 1986 publication were printed and the document was translated into 12 languages (WHO, 1990).

Following the release of *Cancer Pain Relief* in 1986, France and Japan adopted policies for the care of the terminally ill; Australia, France, Japan and Sweden adopted policies for pain control; and Italy and some States of India made provision for morphine to be available by oral administration. A WHO demonstration project, the Wisconsin Cancer Pain Initiative, was established in America and WHO staff and collaborators addressed numerous conferences and workshops in relation to *Cancer Pain Relief* and the work of the WHO. WHO Collaborating Centres were established in Amsterdam (quality of life), Milan (cancer pain and palliative care), Oxford (palliative care) and Wisconsin (symptom evaluation), with three further centres established later in New York (cancer pain research and education), Saitama (cancer pain relief and quality of life) and Winnipeg (quality of life in cancer care).

---

**Box 1.1: Definition of palliative care**

*Palliative care*
- Affirms life and regards dying as a normal process
- Neither hastens nor postpones death
- Provides relief from pain and other distressing symptoms
- Integrates the psychological and spiritual aspects of patient care
- Offers a support system to help patients live as actively as possible until death
- Offers a support system to help the family cope during the patient's illness and in their own bereavement

From WHO, 1990, p.11

---

No doubt due to the way in which the work of these centres raised the profile of palliative care, in 1990 the WHO published *Pain Relief and Palliative Care*, a report of a further WHO Expert Committee. This report built on the original publication, but focused significantly on the concept of palliative care, which it defined for the first time in this document. Since then, a number of amendments have occurred but the essence of the definition is unchanged.

*Palliative care is the active total care of patients whose disease is not responsive to curative treatment. Control of pain, of other symptoms, and of psychological, social and spiritual problems is paramount. The goal of palliative care is achievement of the best possible quality of life for patients and their families. Many aspects of palliative care are also applicable earlier in the course of the illness, in conjunction with anticancer treatment (WHO, 2004a).*

One of the earliest definitions was that provided by the WHO in 1990 (see *Box 1.1*).

This focus on palliative care was a significant philosophical shift from the first WHO document released in 1986 which focused almost exclusively on the assessment and management of pain. The 1990 WHO report still addressed cancer pain but within a palliative care framework, setting the scene with the definition of palliative care. In addition the publication provided information not only about cancer pain, but also about opioid availability, other common symptoms of cancer patients, psychosocial and spiritual considerations, ethical issues, and education and training. The document then went into some detail about the need for national approaches to palliative care, and made a number of recommendations both to the WHO and the member states in relation to the information provided.

## Ethical and legal issues

This emphasis on care of the dying was developing concurrently with huge technological developments in resuscitation and intensive care, meaning that life could be extended, potentially indefinitely, by artificial means (Chiarella, 2000). No doubt as a result of the emphasis on dying with dignity, significant ethical and legal issues, including court cases, were arising in relation to the appropriate time to discontinue treatment, when to decide a person was dying or indeed dead, and when palliative care ought to be instituted instead of resuscitative therapy. In the late 1980s the Hastings Center, a specialist centre in philosophy and bioethics in America, published a report entitled *Guidelines on the Termination of Life-Sustaining Treatment and the Care of the Dying* (1987). These guidelines, while expressly stating that they had no legal status and did not set out to develop 'cookbook medicine' (p.2), nevertheless made a number of unequivocal statements which had been troubling the healthcare professional community for some time.

Although these issues will be discussed in more detail in *Chapters 2 and 3*, the guidelines rejected the distinction between ordinary and extraordinary means of sustaining life, rejected the distinction between withholding and withdrawing life-sustaining treatment and made clear the patient's right to autonomy in decisions about end-of-life treatment and care. Furthermore, the guidelines emphasised the responsibility of healthcare professionals to provide supportive or palliative care for dying patients in whom further treatment would be a greater burden than a benefit (Hastings Center, 1987). These guidelines were expressly acknowledged as being the foundation for the *Appleton International Consensus Statement on Developing Guidelines for Decisions to Forgo Life-Prolonging Treatment*, first published in the *Journal of the Danish Medical Association (Ugeskr Laeger)* in 1989. Following feedback from previously unrepresented countries, the guidelines were reprinted as a broader consensus statement in the *Journal of Medical Ethics* in 1992 (Stanley, 1989, 1992).

## The 'data-driven' phase

Throughout this time, hospice care continued to be delivered to standards of excellence overall, but there did not seem to be any significant expansion of the concept into the mainstream healthcare delivery systems. To date, the development of policy on end-of-life care, while having the needs of patients suffering from terminal illness (predominantly cancer) as its major goal, had focused on the work of governments and legislators and the practice of health professionals. Similarly, health professionals (predominantly doctors), in struggling with ethical and legal issues surrounding end-of-life care, had worked together to provide guidance and advice on how best to manage these problems. Despite these efforts, it became apparent that many people, even in developed countries, were not receiving the type of end-of-life care envisaged either by the WHO or by the key groups of healthcare professionals developing ethical guidelines. In the mid-1990s, there was a change in emphasis and, certainly in the developed world, a shift in the dynamics of power, as the consumer focus gained momentum. This period has been described by Christopher (2003, p.105) as the 'data-driven phase'.

The American Study to Understand Prognoses and Preferences for Outcomes and Risks of Treatment (SUPPORT) was 'a prospective cohort study at five major university hospitals of outcomes, preferences and decision makers in seriously ill hospitalised adults and their families' (SUPPORT Principal Investigators, 1995). Phase I of this study set out to evaluate five outcomes in order to describe the medical decision making process. These outcomes were: incidence and timing of written do-not-resuscitate (DNR) orders, patient/physician agreement on cardio-pulmonary resuscitation (CPR) preferences; the number of days in intensive care (ICU) comatose or receiving ventilator support prior to death; severity of pain experienced; and use of hospital resources (Counsell *et al*, 2003). The study involved 4301 seriously ill patients, and demonstrated that 46% of DNR orders were written within two days of the patients' deaths; 47% of physicians were not aware of their patients' preferences regarding CPR; 38% of patients who died spent 10 days or more in ICU prior to their death and moderate or severe pain was suffered by 50% of patients who died in hospital for at least half of the time during their last days (Byock, 2001).

Following these results, Phase II of the study used expertly trained nurses to provide advice and education to patients around end-of-life issues and procedures and to act as a conduit between patients and physicians, informing physicians about patients' prognoses, symptoms and preferences for care. This well-constructed intervention produced no measurable changes in clinical outcomes. When this research was first published in 1995, it was clear that there were differences between end-of-life care in hospices and the quality of care patients were receiving in the traditional hospital setting. The Institute of Medicine (IOM) confirmed these findings in the *Report of the IOM Committee on Care at the End of Life* in 1997. The IOM Report recommended a mixed-management model (MMM) of end-of-life care. This MMM proposes that active, life-prolonging treatment should occur simultaneously with preparation for death and dying, so that people with a potentially terminal illness are well prepared throughout their treatment process, rather than there being a significant shift of emphasis at the end of life (Glare and Virik, 2001).

At the same time in England, the Department of Health published the report of the Expert Advisory Group on Cancer, *A Policy Framework for Commissioning Cancer Services: Report to the CMOs for England and Wales* (the Calman-Hine Report). This report was written in response to concerns about differences in the outcomes for cancer care across the country and made a range of recommendations about cancer care and palliative and terminal care, and emphasised the importance of a palliative care approach (Mathew *et al*, 2003). It noted particularly that 'hospice units have sometimes developed in an ad hoc fashion through voluntary efforts and fundraising. As a result, links with health authorities and purchasers are under-developed in some areas' (Calman-Hine Report, 1995). In Wales the Cameron Report recommended similar policy changes to support cancer management (Welsh Office, 1996). These two reports influenced the policy framework for cancer care that has since been set out in the *NHS Cancer Plan*, significantly subtitled *A Plan for Investment, a Plan for Reform* (Department of Health, 2000), which recommended (*inter alia*) the establishment of cancer networks to ensure continuity of care.

In America, the philanthropic sector mobilised to drive the policy agenda on end-of-life care. The Robert Wood Johnson Foundation (RWJF) established the Last Acts Campaign, which has published a range of documents related to end-of-life care (Christopher, 2003) and funded numerous education programmes and workshops for healthcare professionals and the public (Ackermann, 2000; Rushton and Sabatier, 2001). One of its most recent publications was a less than glowing State by State 'report card' on end-of-life care (Anon, 2003). The RWJF has worked closely on these activities with the Open Society Institute, a network of foundations created and founded by the philanthropist George Soros, which established the Project on Death in America (PDIA), that has also been centrally involved in producing lobby documents and educating healthcare professionals (Mathew *et al*, 2003; Price, 2003). The public debate on dying in America was taken into the living rooms of Americans as a result of the public television series *On Our Own Terms*, a documentary produced by Bill Moyers. These developments have triggered significant 'consumer-centric' changes to legislation and policy in America, which will be discussed in *Chapters 2 and 3*.

In England, other distinctly European forces were also driving a health consumer focus on patient care. In October 2000, the Human Rights Act (UK) 1998 was proclaimed, which incorporated the majority of the substantive rights identified in the European Convention on Human Rights into the UK legal system. This effectively means that people who believe their rights to have been violated by a 'public authority' will now be able to seek redress through the UK Courts, instead of having to take such a case to the European Court of Human Rights in Strasbourg. This has significant implications for health consumer rights as the term 'public authority' includes the Department of Health, health authorities, health trusts and all other public healthcare providers. Consequently employees of these public authorities will be expected by law to observe the European Convention on Human Rights obligations under the Act and will be expected to be able to demonstrate that they have done so. While the Committee on Medical Ethics of the British Medical Association was quick to point out that the 'requirements of the Human Rights Act reflect, very closely, existing good practice', it also acknowledged that 'many doctors are not accustomed to thinking in terms of "rights"'. The Committee further advised that, while the Human Rights Act might not alter the final decision, 'the way in which the decision is reached will differ (by specifically considering human rights) and there will be greater transparency and scrutiny of the decision making process' (Committee on Medical Ethics, 2000, p.2).

## The ongoing need for improved access to opioids

On a wider international scale, the WHO was continuing its campaign to improve opioid availability. In 1996, the WHO Expert Advisory Committee on Cancer Pain Relief and Active Supportive Care reissued its advisory booklet on pain management with an additional guide to opioid availability (WHO, 1996). The publication was 'intended for use by both drug regulators and healthcare workers and to promote communication between the two groups' (p.41). The booklet sets out five rules for the use of analgesics in cancer pain: by mouth, by the clock, by the ladder (the WHO pain management ladder), for the individual, and attention to detail. The WHO sought a review of the information in the second part of the booklet on opioid availability from the International Narcotics Control Board (INCB), the body responsible for administering the Single Convention on Narcotic Drugs, and from 10 national drug regulatory authorities. The WHO Expert Advisory Committee identified five major impediments to cancer pain relief. These were:

- Absence of national policies on cancer pain relief and palliative care.
- Lack of awareness on the part of healthcare workers, policy makers and administrators and the public that most cancer pain can be relieved.
- Shortage of financial resources and limitations of healthcare delivery systems and personnel.
- Concern that medical use of opioids will produce psychological dependence and drug abuse.
- Legal restrictions on the use and availability of opioid analgesics.

In response to these impediments, the WHO advocated a strategy with the following three key components: national or state policies that support cancer pain relief through government endorsement of education and drug availability; education for the public, health personnel and regulators; and modifications of laws and regulations to improve the availability of drugs, especially the opioid analgesics (WHO, 1996). There follows a detailed account of the approaches and activities needed to implement the key components of the strategy. Following on from this publication, the WHO ran a series of workshops in countries all over the world, which significantly impacted on international development in palliative and end-of-life care.

As a result of feedback from these workshops, which clarified the ongoing needs of countries in relation to these three key components, the WHO developed a number of supportive and advisory documents, three of which are of particular significance to this review. The first, *Achieving Balance in National Opioids Control Policy* (WHO, 2000) provided a set of assessment guidelines for countries in order to benchmark their success and to identify further improvements that could be made to their national opioid availability. The second, *National Cancer Control Programmes: Policies and Managerial Guidelines* (WHO, 2002) was developed in collaboration with the International Union Against Cancer, and provided advice to countries and organisations on developing national cancer control programmes. The third, *Palliative Care: Symptom Management and End-of-Life Care: Integrated Management of Adolescent and Adult Illness* (WHO, 2003b) is a detailed and practical procedure manual on care of the dying, one of four manuals developed to assist first level healthcare workers with the care of people dying with HIV/AIDS.

As an example of national developments in line with the WHO Guidelines, the Drug Enforcement Agency in the USA, which administers the Federal Controlled Substance Act (1970), issued a joint policy statement in 2001, with 21 health organisations involved in pain management improvement, entitled *Promoting Pain Relief and Preventing Abuse of Pain Medications: A Critical Balancing Act*. This document has since been endorsed by a total of 44 health organisations. In addition, the American Joint Commission on Accreditation of Health Care Organizations (JCAHO), which accredits over 19000 healthcare facilities, now requires accredited facilities to have policies and procedures in place to assure that pain is assessed and managed appropriately (Dahl, 2002).

In 2004, the UK Pain Society published two documents, one for the public and one for all healthcare professionals concerned with the use of opioids in the management of persistent non-cancer pain. The first publication *Opioid Medications for Persistent Pain: Information for Patients* (Pain Society, 2004a) is an information leaflet about opioids for persistent painful conditions that has been prepared for patients and their paid and unpaid carers. The second document *Recommendations for the Appropriate Use of Opioids for Persistent Non-Cancer Pain* (Pain Society, 2004b) makes recommendations to help to define the appropriate use of opioids in such circumstances. The recommendations were produced for use in both primary and secondary care, and provide a national framework to support the appropriate use of opioids. They encourage local liaison between primary care, pain and drug services, eg. drug information services, and addiction services.

# Widening the focus of palliative and end-of-life care

In the policy documents developed since the beginning of the twenty-first century there is a widening in the focus of palliative care, not only in terms of the time when palliative care ought to be instituted, but also in terms of those people who ought to deliver palliative care and those people who ought to be recipients. The extension of the palliative care time-frame was first raised in the WHO 1990 publication *Pain Relief and Palliative Care*, since the definition included the recommendation that 'many aspects of palliative care are also applicable earlier in the course of the illness, in conjunction with anticancer treatment' (p.11). This has led to terms such as 'end-of-life care' and also 'terminal care' being used to describe the period immediately before death.

The need for palliative care to be widened from a specialist hospice service has been a constant theme since the mid-1990s, when studies such as the SUPPORT study identified that acute hospitals were not delivering care to the dying in the same way that hospice care was provided. Internationally, education programmes have since provided palliative care education to a wide range of healthcare providers, including first level workers (WHO, 2003b), hospital-based generalist nurses (Rushton and Sabatier, 2001), hospital-based generalist doctors (Ackermann, 2000), and community nurses (Simpson, 2003). The National Institute for Clinical Excellence (NICE) in March 2004 published a manual or guidance on cancer services entitled *Improving Supportive and Palliative Care for Adults with Cancer*. The manual goes into considerable detail about the need for palliative care to be able to be delivered by all healthcare staff, whether generalist or specialist.

In terms of extending the need for palliative care to groups other than cancer sufferers, there have been a number of relatively recent publications either demonstrating the extent to which this might be occurring or lobbying for its further extension. In response to the ongoing tragedy of the spread of HIV/AIDS in Africa, the WHO instituted a two-stage project in 1995 to improve palliative care for people dying with AIDS. The report on this community project in five countries in sub-Saharan Africa, which focuses on palliative care for the many people dying of HIV/AIDS in Africa, in addition to those dying of cancer, was published in 2004 (WHO, 2004b). Despite significant infrastructure and educational support for health workers to date, only Botswana of the five countries involved had incorporated palliative care services into its public health system, and access to opioids in all countries was still difficult.

In 2004, three European documents were published which address the need for improved palliative care for older people (WHO, 2004a; 2004c; EURAG, 2004). In response to changing demographics, the WHO Europe document *Palliative Care: The Solid Facts* (2004a) sets out to provide simple, understandable evidence for health policy and decision makers. It makes the argument that health services should provide good quality palliative care for all people facing serious chronic illness. It goes on to 'provide evidence for the effectiveness of palliative care, show how it can be improved, and explain the need to ensure full access' (p.i). The booklet also explores the varied cultural and healthcare contexts in different countries, and stresses the importance of education for healthcare professionals.

WHO Europe also produced a companion booklet entitled *Better Palliative Care for Older People* that explores the needs of the elderly in more detail. The companion booklet highlights the fact that the main predicted causes of death for 2020, ranked for prevalence, are ischaemic heart disease, cerebrovascular disease, chronic obstructive pulmonary disease, lower respiratory tract infections, with lung, trachea and bronchial cancer ranking only as fifth. The document points out that heart failure affects more than one in 10 people aged over 70, and the five-year mortality of over 80% is worse than for many cancers. Dementia is also specifically mentioned as a disease that is only just beginning to be recognised as a terminal illness, with the median length of survival from diagnosis to death being just eight years.

WHO Europe is explicit in its stated aims that both booklets seek to broaden awareness, stimulate debate and promote action. Perhaps the most critical difference between these two documents and earlier documents is that they call for palliative care to be treated in future as a public health issue. This is because the changing demographics of the ageing population means that the need for palliative care is going to reach epidemic proportions, due to the significant projected increase of chronic life-threatening disease in future ageing populations.

In frank recognition of the aims of these documents, EURAG, the European Federation of Older Persons, followed on by producing a lobby document entitled *Making Palliative Care a Priority Topic on the European Health Agenda* and by making recommendations for the development of palliative care in Europe. In her introduction, the Director of EURAG, Gertraud Daye, makes it clear that EURAG has learnt lessons on lobbying and policy development from the editors of the WHO reports in Europe and the Open Society Institute of the Soros Foundation in America. These lessons weave together the threads of policy and philanthropic initiatives that have predominated within the history of policy development in end-of-life care. EURAG adopts a new style from previous policy documents and drafts up a proposal for a decision of the Council of the European Union. The style is a replica of the decision documents of the Council and is worthy of repetition in *Box 1.2*, as its content undoubtedly sets the tone for the focus of future policy documents.

Documents currently being produced in England also acknowledge the need to extend palliative care beyond cancer. The Executive Summary of the NICE Manual (2004) makes the point that, although the document is focused solely

## Box 1.2: EURAG draft decision document for the Council of the European Union

The Council of the European Union

- Bearing in mind that every human being has to die
- Knowing that for some people the last phase of life is filled with great suffering and that older persons in particular are affected
- Knowing that organised palliative care can bring relief through excellent symptom control and psychosocial care and offering assistance to family members
- Taking into consideration the recommendations of the Committee of Ministers of the Council of Europe to member States on 'the organisation of palliative care' (adopted on 12 November 2003)
- Taking into consideration the work and the recommendations of the WHO Europe Collaboration Projects 'Better Palliative Care for Older People' and 'Palliative Care and the Solid Facts'
- Being convinced that effective measures in all political fields have to be supported to raise awareness about the needs of terminally ill older persons and the knowledge of possible solutions
- Recognising that the access to appropriate and efficient care will become increasingly important in the future in particular for older persons
- Recognising that the collaboration of volunteers is of particular importance in care patterns oriented towards patients and family members
- Recognising that population ageing and the implications it presents for palliative care are major public health issues for the twenty-first century

Requests the Member States
- To pay more attention to the importance of preventing avoidable suffering of terminally ill people and to ensure that these problems are adequately considered
- To take into consideration the implementation of these recommendations of the Committee of Ministers to Member States on the organisation of palliative care of the Council of Europe at national level

Requests the Commission
- To put special emphasis on active collaboration in questions concerning palliative care
- To take measures for facilitating the exchange of information and mutual learning in the framework of national policies in order to improve palliative care
- To initiate a periodic report on the situation of palliative care for older persons

From Council of the European Union, 2004, p.8

on services for adult patients with cancer and their families, 'it may inform the development of service models for other groups of patients'. The Pain Society publications also recognise and promote the need for opioids for persistent non-cancer pain (Pain Society, 2004a, 2004b).

## Conclusion

Policy development in relation to palliative and end-of-life care has changed significantly since the origins of palliative care as a 'boutique' specialist area of hospice care in the 1960s and 1970s. International agencies such as the WHO have shifted the emphasis away from the care of solely cancer patients (although cancer patients still feature significantly) to a much broader definition of palliative care. This broader emphasis encompasses people with life-shortening illnesses who are not going to die immediately, but who still need to plan for death while undergoing life-prolonging treatment. This includes people with diseases other than cancer, particularly HIV/AIDS in developing countries; and most recently, older people, who will be much more likely to die of chronic heart and lung diseases and dementia in the future. The changing population demographics in the developed world have also stimulated a call for palliative and end-of-life care for older people to be considered as a public health issue.

There has been a surge in consumer involvement in palliative and end-of-life care, and an increasing amount of research into patients' and families' experiences at the end of life, much (although not all) of which has not been positive. The philanthropic sector has funded significant projects and ongoing education in this area.

Finally, the problem of opioid availability for the management of pain remains unresolved, although some inroads have been made due to collaboration between national and international drug control agencies and healthcare deliverers.

A timeline for the major policy documents is shown in *Table 1.1*. In the ensuing chapters many of the issues which have been touched upon within some of these policy documents will be expanded in detail.

| | | |
|---|---|---|
| **Table 1.1. Timeline of key policy documents discussed** | | |
| **Year** | **Document** | **Author** |
| 1961 | *Single Convention on Narcotic Drugs (amended 1972)* | UN |
| 1986 | *Cancer Pain Relief* | WHO |
| 1987 | *Guidelines on the Termination of Life-Sustaining Treatment and the Care of the Dying* | *Hastings Center |
| 1990 | *Pain Relief and Palliative Care* | WHO |
| 1995 | *American Study to Understand Prognoses and Preferences for Outcomes and Risks of Treatment (SUPPORT)* | *SUPPORT Principal Investigators |
| 1995 | *A policy framework for commissioning cancer services: Report to the CMOs for England and Wales (The Calman-Hine Report)* | DOH (England) |
| 1996 | *The Cameron Report* | Welsh Office |
| 1996 | *Cancer Pain Relief (2nd edn) with a guide to opioid availability* | WHO |
| 1997 | *Report of the IOM Committee on care at the end of life* | *US Institute of Medicine |
| 1998 | *Withholding and Withdrawing Life-Prolonging Treatment: Guidance for Decision-Making* | *BMA |
| 2000 | *NHS Cancer Plan* | DOH (England) |
| 2000 | *Achieving Balance in National Opioids Control Policy* | WHO |
| 2001 | *Promoting Pain Relief and Preventing Abuse of Pain Medications: A Critical Balancing Act* | US Drug Enforcement Agency |
| 2002 | *National Cancer Control Programmes: International Policies and Managerial Guidelines* | WHO, UICC |
| 2002 | *Withholding and Withdrawing Life-Prolonging Treatments: Good Practice in Decision-Making* | *GMC (UK) |
| 2002 | *Making Decisions: Helping People Who Have Difficulty Deciding for Themselves* | LCD DCA (UK) |
| 2002 | *National Cancer Control Programs: Policies and Managerial Guidelines* | WHO |
| 2003 | *Global Action Against Cancer* | WHO |
| 2003 | *Decisions Relating to Cardiopulmonary Resuscitation* | *BMA, RCN Resuscitation Council (UK) |

| | | |
|---|---|---|
| 2003 | *Palliative Care: Symptom Management and End-of-Life Care: Integrated Management of Adolescent and Adult Illness* | WHO |
| 2004 | *Opioid Medications for Persistent Pain: Information for Patients* | Pain Society (UK) |
| 2004 | *Recommendations for the Appropriate Use of Opioids for Persistent Non-Cancer Pain* | Pain Society (UK) |
| 2004 | *Improving Supportive and Palliative Care for Adults with Cancer* | NICE |
| 2004 | *A Community Health Approach to Palliative Care for HIV and Cancer* | WHO |
| 2004 | *Palliative Care: The Solid Facts* | WHO: Europe |
| 2004 | *Better Palliative Care for Older People* | WHO: Europe |
| 2004 | *Making Palliative Care a Priority Topic on the European Health Agenda and Recommendations the Development of Palliative Care in Europe* | *EURAG, |
| 2004 | *Supportive and Palliative Research in the UK: Report of the NCRI Strategic Planning Group on Supportive and Palliative Care* | NCRI |

*Although these organisations/lobby groups cannot strictly be said to produce policy documents, the documents are included in the timeline because they have been highly influential on policy and/or case law development.

BMA, British Medical Association; DCA, Department for Constitutional Affairs; DOH, Department of Health; EURAG, European Federation of Older Persons; GMC, General Medical Council; LCD, Lord Chancellor's Department; NCRI, National Cancer Research Institute; RCN, Royal College of Nursing; UICC, International Union Against Cancer; UN, United Nations; WHO, World Health Organisation.

# CHAPTER 2

# Legal and ethical issues: Personhood

## Introduction

This chapter provides an overview of the legal and ethical frameworks in which the palliative and end-of-life care debates are situated. The chapter cannot and does not provide definitive legal advice, but explores the legal and ethical issues that inform policy development from an international perspective, selecting key developments from around the world that have impacted the debate on and practice of palliative and end-of-life care. While the issues are of necessity discussed separately within this chapter, in clinical practice many of the issues overlap. Many advisory documents (eg. American Academy of Paediatrics, 1994; British Medical Association, 1998; General Medical Council, 2002; British Medical Association, Resuscitation Council and Royal College of Nursing, 2003) recommend the processes for dealing with end-of-life care decision making from a clinical procedural context and then provide a short overview of the case law and legal framework separately.

The approach this chapter takes is first to explore the increasing legal emphases on patients' rights and autonomy within the law, then to examine the concept of capacity. Advance directives and proxy decision making will also be considered. *Chapter 3* will then examine the therapeutic or practice dilemmas arising from these issues.

## The emphasis on the patient's right to decide

In 1914 Cardozo J made the (since) oft-quoted remark in the case of *Schloendorff* v **Society of New York** 'every human being of adult years and sound mind has a right to determine what shall be done with his own body'. This recognition of the rights of individuals to control what happens to their bodies is a principle of the common law that has long been protected by actions in trespass to the person, specifically actions in battery. In the past 30 years this right has been increasingly exercised in the healthcare arena, and is now an accepted tenet of health law. Bix observed "these judgements (sic) were grounded in the common law position that unconsented-to medical treatment, like other unconsented-to touchings, is an assault or battery, and therefore patients have a presumptive right to refuse medical treatment' (Bix 1995, p.408). In 2002 the Lord Chancellor's Department within the Department for Constitutional Affairs published a consultation paper entitled *Making Decisions: Helping People who Have Difficulty Deciding for Themselves* (Department for Constitutional Affairs. 2002a). Part of this paper was a series of leaflets aimed at various professional groups and the public. Leaflet 2, *A Guide for Health Care Professionals*, begins by stating that 'a key principle of the law is that every adult has the right to make their own decisions and must be assumed to have capacity to do so unless it is proven otherwise'. It continues, 'this principle applies equally to healthcare and treatment decisions. Patients have a right to determine what happens to their own bodies and valid consent must be obtained if the person is able to give it before starting treatment. Some patients may need help and support to be able to give, or refuse, consent' (Department for Constitutional Affairs. 2002b).

At this juncture it seems apposite to point out that in healthcare policy the concept of the right to refuse treatment only becomes an issue when treatment is so abundant that it is there to be refused. In contrast with developing countries, the debate about the right to refuse treatment suggests that potentially curative treatment, whether effective or not, may be ongoing until death unless refused. Thus the case law and legislation concerning the right to refuse treatment is very much a construct of the developed world. As was seen in *Chapter 1*, the issues concerning developing countries are not whether patients are able to refuse treatment, but whether they are able to access it.

Concerns about being able to determine the course of treatment, particularly in the face of medical futility at the end of life, have arisen in conjunction with medicine's ability to extend life. The challenge has been to decide whether, just because more could be done, more should be done to prolong a patient's life, if the burden of the proposed therapy outweighed the benefits. As medicine developed throughout the twentieth century, healthcare practitioners found it difficult to forgo life-prolonging treatment and continued to treat the patient's condition aggressively until death, thus depriving the patient of the opportunity for appropriate palliative or end-of-life care (Burt, 2000).

The growing health consumer movement, exemplified by the Community–State Partnerships to Improve End-of-Life Care, funded by the RWJF (Christopher, 2003) has meant that more people are aware of what palliative and end-of-life care have to offer, and thus more challenges are being made to the courts when care is not delivered in the way health consumers wish. Similarly, some of the more extreme activist groups, such as those advocating for euthanasia and physician-assisted suicide, have brought the debate about the potential for and problems with end-of-life care into the mainstream, even if the public are not necessarily in accord with the goals of such groups (Blacksher and Christopher, 2002). However, the issue that first brought the question of the right to refuse treatment at the end of life into the legal domain was the difficulty for people who were no longer able to refuse treatment for themselves.

## Developments in America

The earliest 'right to refuse treatment' case to gain significant attention was the 1976 case of Karen Ann Quinlan, a young woman in a persistent vegetative state (PVS), whose parents sought the right to act as surrogate decision makers and to refuse mechanical ventilation for their daughter. A PVS is one where the patient is left with irrecoverable brain damage, although the clinical state manifests as long periods of open-eyed wakefulness that alternates with sleep, inability to utter words, and presence of limb spasticity (Taylor, 1997). In *Re Quinlan* the Supreme Court of New Jersey granted the parents the right to act in the capacity of surrogate decision-makers, stating that they might use their 'substituted judgment' for the judgment of their daughter. In 1983 the Californian Court of Appeal heard the case of *Barber* v *Superior Court* where a group of physicians had been charged with murder because, with permission of the parents, they had removed artificial nutrition and hydration from a comatose patient. The Court held that the physicians had not committed an unlawful act and accepted the principle of substituted judgment. The Court also dismissed the distinction between 'extraordinary' and 'ordinary' means as a strategy for classifying medical interventions and recommended that medical interventions should be evaluated by the benefits and burdens they conferred on a patient (Luce and Alpers, 2001). In the 1985 New Jersey case of *Re Conroy*, the extent to which a medical treatment might become a burden was eloquently described:

> *Pervasive bodily intrusions ... will arouse feeling akin to humiliation and mortification for the helpless patient. When cherished values of human dignity and personal privacy, which belong to every person, living or dying, are sufficiently transgressed by what is being done to the individual, we should be ready to say: enough.*

*Re Conroy [1985]* provided a description of the test for 'best interests' which is still considered the most influential description today (Luce and Alpers, 2001). The Court in Conroy would only apply the best interests test where there was no reliable evidence of the patient's wishes. The test had two elements: that the burden of the patient's life with treatment must outweigh the benefits to the patient of continued life and that the recurring, unavoidable pain of the patient's life with treatment must be such that administering the treatment is inhumane.

However, the American courts were not prepared to give carte blanche surrogate decision making powers to patients' families. In 1990 the United States Supreme Court was asked to determine the case of *Cruzan* v *Director, Missouri Department of Health*, in which the parents of a young woman who was in a PVS following an automobile accident in 1983 sought to discontinue her artificial feeding through a gastrostomy tube. The parents argued that Nancy Cruzan had made statements during her life to the effect that she would not want to live life 'as a vegetable'. The State hospital officials refused to terminate the treatment, arguing that they were bound to preserve human life. The question put to the Supreme Court was whether the State's refusal to terminate her life support system violated the Cruzans' Fourteenth Amendment right to due process and liberty interests (ie. their individual freedoms) by blocking their right to refuse unwanted medical treatment. Because Cruzan was a Supreme Court decision, it became binding on all of the American States, unlike Quinlan, which was a decision of a State Supreme Court (ie. New Jersey).

In a six to three decision, the Supreme Court held that a person did have a liberty interest under the due process clause of the Fourteenth Amendment and ought to be able to refuse unwanted medical treatment, provided they were competent and there was 'clear and convincing evidence' the person did not want artificial support to keep them alive. As Mareiniss (2005, p.235) observes, 'Cruzan established the right to refuse medical care was a constitutionally protected liberty interest'. However, the Supreme Court did not accept that the standard for 'clear and convincing evidence' was met in this case. Further, the Supreme Court distinguished between the requirement for clear and convincing evidence and the concept of substituted judgment, stating that the 'Due process clause does not require the State to accept the "substituted judgment" clause in the absence of substantial proof that their views reflect the patient's'. The safeguard of the requirement for substantial proof was a balance between the liberty interests of the patient on the one hand and the State's interest in protecting life on the other (Mareiniss, 2005). As a footnote, it is reported that, following this personal disappointment for the Cruzan family, they moved their daughter to another State where the feeding tube was removed and she died (Goldberg, 2002).

In December 1991, the US Federal Government implemented the Patient Self-Determination Act (US) 1990 which, *inter alia*, required health maintenance organisations to inform all adults about advance directives, defined within the Act as 'written instructions, such as a living will or durable power of attorney for healthcare, recognised under State law ... and relating to the provision of care when the individual is incapacitated' (Roff, 2001). Since then, the Supreme Court affirmed its support for the forgoing of life-prolonging medical treatment in two 1997 cases, *Washington* v *Glucksberg* and *Vacco* v *Quill*, both cases dealing with the constitutionality of laws prohibiting physician-assisted suicide (which will be further discussed in *Chapter 3*). In Glucksberg, the

Court followed Cruzan in confirming the right of competent patients to refuse treatment. However, it differentiated between the liberty interest in refusing treatment and any liberty interest in either committing suicide or being assisted to commit suicide. The Court pronounced that, to find for the respondents (as opposed to the State), it would have to 'reverse centuries of legal doctrine and practice, and strike down the considered policy choice of almost every State'.

In Vacco, the Court went into some detail about the difference between refusal of treatment and assisted suicide. 'Everyone, regardless of physical condition, is entitled, if competent, to refuse unwanted lifesaving medical treatment; no one is permitted to assist a suicide'. In both these judgments the Supreme Court used the doctrine of double effect (to be discussed in *Chapter 3*) to distinguish assisted suicide from palliative care and went so far as to suggest that, if any State legislated to interfere with the appropriate administration of analgesia to the dying, it would be prepared to mandate patient access to palliative care (Luce and Alpers, 2001). Note the use of 'almost' every State in the quote from the Glucksberg judgment. This must refer to the fact that in 1997, the same year as the Glucksberg judgment, Oregon passed its Death with Dignity Act, legalising physician-assisted suicide (PAS). This will be discussed further in *Chapter 3*. However, notwithstanding the debate around palliative care and PAS, it is clear that the right of a competent person to refuse life-prolonging treatment is established at law, even in advance, providing there is clear and convincing evidence of his or her wishes.

The *Re Schiavo* saga is the most recent to explore the question of proof of an individual's wishes surrounding end of life and also to highlight the relationship between medicine, the courts and the legislature. This remarkable and tragic series of decisions concerns Terri Schiavo, a young woman in a PVS since 1990 following a myocardial infarction at the age of 27, the management of which resulted in anoxic brain damage. She is described clinically as having had 'severe hypoxic-ischaemic encephalopathy, with no evidence of higher cortical function [and] ... severe atrophy of her cerebral hemispheres [on computed tomography scan]' (Quill, 2005, p.1630). Her husband and guardian, Michael Schiavo, filed a malpractice suit on her behalf and won over $1 million in damages, after which the parents contested his guardianship and filed an unsuccessful petition to remove him as guardian. In 1998, in the first of a series of *Re Schiavo* cases, Michael successfully petitioned a Florida trial court, based on the evidence of her verbal wishes to him and the fact that she was in a PVS, to remove Terri's gastrotomy feeding tube (g-tube) and discontinue hydration.

Terri's parents, the Schindlers, protested the original petition and appealed the decision on three grounds. Firstly, that Michael was having a relationship with another woman, although still married to Terri; and secondly, that Michael had a conflict of interest as Terri's guardian as he stood to profit from Terri's death because the malpractice settlement would revert to him. Thirdly, they argued that, because Terri was a Catholic, her religion would testify to her desire to live, thus refuting Michael's argument that Terri had indicated she would not have wanted to continue to live in such a condition. Unfortunately, there was no advance directive to assist the court. The religious issues in this case became a *cause celebre* (Quill, 2005), with the Schindlers enlisting the support of 'vocal and organised ... conservative religious organisations' to promote their case to the various State and Federal Governments (Annas, 2005).

In 2001, the Florida appellate court affirmed the order to discontinue nutrition and hydration, agreed there was no need to appoint a guardian *ad litem* and did not criticise the court for finding clear and convincing evidence of Terri's intent, despite conflicting evidence from the parents and no advance directive. This was in contrast to the Cruzan case where, despite the family being unanimous in its evidence that Nancy Cruzan would not have wanted to live in such a condition, there was held to be no clear and convincing evidence of her wishes.

Three more appeals followed, all of which were unsuccessful. In the fourth appeal, the Schindlers requested a *de novo* review, which was declined. In October 2003, the Governor of Florida, Jeb Bush, ordered a stay of the trial court's order allowing Terri's nutrition and hydration to be discontinued. A statute was enacted (2003-418) known popularly as Terri's Law, because it applied specifically and only to Terri. Its constitutionality was immediately challenged and in the autumn of 2004 the Florida Supreme Court ruled Terri's Law unconstitutional. This ruling was because the statute contravened the doctrine of the separation of powers, which states that the three branches of government, ie. executive, legislature and judiciary, cannot encroach upon each other's powers (Annas, 2005).

Governor Bush appealed the decision of the Florida Supreme Court but in January 2005 the US Supreme Court refused to hear the appeal. On the strength of this Supreme Court decision the Florida trial judge ordered the removal of the g-tube in 30 days, which would set the date and time for removal as 1pm on Friday 18 March 2005. The Schindlers, again with the support of religious and right-to-life advocates, sought a range of appeals and reviews, all of which were unsuccessful. At this point, an event that has been described as 'unique in American politics' (Annas, 2005, p.1713) occurred:

*After more than a week of discussion, and after formally declaring their Easter recess without action, Congress reconvened two days after the feeding tube was removed to consider emergency legislation designed to apply only to Terri Schiavo.*

The US Senate delayed the Easter recess and the house suspended its rules and adopted a Bill 'for the relief of the parents of Theresa Marie Schiavo' which was passed by a four-to-one margin early in the morning of 21 March 2005 (Charatan, 2005a). President Bush returned early from his weekend break in Texas to sign the Bill at 1.11am. This measure granted the federal courts the power to review the case without weighing previous judicial findings. However, the federal courts did not make new findings but rather confirmed that the removal of the g-tube was lawful and justified. Terri Schiavo died on 31 March 2005 (Gostin, 2005). Autopsy showed that she had been in a severe PVS, with her brain atrophied to half its size and her vision centres dead, rendering her totally blind (Charatan, 2005b). Despite the remarkable interventions by both executive and legislature, and the fact that the diagnosis of PVS was confirmed on autopsy, the decision of the original trial court to accept Michael's evidence of Terri's wishes not to continue living has been criticised as being a departure from previous evidentiary requirements (Mareiniss, 2005). Mareiniss suggests that, despite the purported application of the 'clear and convincing evidence' test in the Schiavo case, the real reason underlying all of the judgments in favour of discontinuation of treatment was in fact, the overwhelming evidence of the futility of continuing to keep Terri alive by artificial hydration and nutrition (p.250).

## Developments in the UK

In the UK, Lord Donaldson addressed the issue of making decisions for incapacitated persons in the 1990 case of *Re J (A Minor) (Wardship: Medical treatment) [1991]* where he applied the 'substituted judgment' test and determined that there was no obligation to give treatment that was burdensome and futile. However, the first decision made by the House of Lords, the highest court in the land, concerning the issue was *Airedale NHS Trust v Bland [1993]* which reviewed the status of Anthony Bland, a 21-year-old man who had been in a PVS for three years after suffering severe crush injuries following the collapse of a stand at the Hillsborough stadium. Anthony Bland was breathing spontaneously and being fed via a naso-gastric tube. Clearly, if he were not fed, he would starve to death, as he was unable to feed himself.

The treating doctor and the parents sought a declaration from the court that the doctor 'may lawfully discontinue all life-sustaining treatment and medical support and thereafter need not furnish medical treatment to [the defendant] except for the sole purpose of enabling [him] to end his life and die peacefully with the greatest dignity and the least of pain, suffering and distress'. The declaration was granted in the High Court and confirmed by the Court of Appeal. The Official Solicitor, in his role as guardian *ad litem*, appealed to the House of Lords asking the broad question 'In what circumstances, if ever, can those having a duty to feed an invalid lawfully stop doing so?' Their Lordships did not answer the question either directly or unanimously, but did confirm the declaration granted by the High Court. Lord Goff of Chieveley stated,

'The principle of the sanctity of human life must yield to the principle of self-determination.' Lord Mustill spelt this latter principle out clearly,

*If the patient is capable of making a decision on whether to permit treatment and decides not to permit it his choice must be obeyed, even if on any objective view it is contrary to his best interests. A doctor has no right to proceed in the face of objection, even if it is plain to all, including the doctor, that adverse consequences and even death will or may ensue.*

This very scenario had been addressed in a Canadian case in 1990. In *Malette* v *Schulman* it was confirmed that a person has the right to refuse treatment even if the refusal might cause him or her serious harm. In this case, a young woman who was a Jehovah's Witness successfully sued for battery after she was given a blood transfusion to save her life when unconscious in contravention of her express written instructions.

In Bland, permission was given to discontinue feeding Anthony, but all the individual judgments recognised the difficulties such decisions raised and two of Their Lordships recommended that parliament should consider the issues involved. A number of committees were established over the ensuing years, notably the House of Lords Select Committee on Medical Ethics in 1994 and the British Medical Association's Committee in 1995. Pursuant to these, in 1999 the Lord Chancellor's Department published a discussion paper on the topic of proxy decision making that was circulated widely for feedback and comment. Following the consultation process by the Lord Chancellor's Department, a document entitled *Making Decisions: Helping People Who Have Difficulty Deciding For Themselves* was published in 2002. This document supported the use of the 'best interests' test (as opposed to the substituted judgment test) as the means to determine whether or not to forgo life-sustaining treatment in the absence of a clear direction. The Lord Chancellor's Department also provided advice to groups of key stakeholders and set out a programme of law reform. The Law Commission had also produced a report and recommendations on mental incapacity and the Lord Chancellor's report adopted some, but not all, of its recommendations for law reform. One accepted set of recommendations was the factors to be taken into consideration when determining a person's best interests. The information is reproduced in full in *Box 2.1*.

Other recent English cases have provided further advice. For example, *Re JT (Adult: Refusal of medical treatment) [1998]*, and *Re AK: Medical treatment: Consent) [2001]* both confirmed the decision of Bland that competent adults may decide to refuse treatment even where refusal might result in harm to themselves or their own death. In *Re MB* v *an NHS Trust [2002]*, it was further determined that doctors have a right to respect a competent refusal of treatment and, where they have an objection to the decision, they have a duty to find another doctor who will carry out the patient's wishes.

---

**Box 2.1. Factors to be taken into consideration in determining 'best interests'\***

*Anything done for, and any decision made on behalf of, a person with incapacity should be done or made in the 'best interests' of that person. In order to assist in deciding what is in a person's best interests, the following should be considered:*

■ The ascertainable past and present wishes and feelings of those concerned, and the factors that person would consider if able to do so.
■ The need to permit and encourage the person to participate or improve his or her ability to participate as fully as possible in anything done for or any decision affecting him or her.
■ The views of other people whom it is appropriate and practical to consult about the person's wishes and beliefs and what would be in his or her best interests.
■ Whether the purpose for which any action or decision is required could be as effectively achieved in a manner less restrictive of the person's freedom of action.
■ Whether there is a reasonable expectation of the person recovering capacity to make the decision in the reasonably foreseeable future.
■ The need to be satisfied that the wishes of the person without capacity were not the result of undue influence.

\*From Department for Constitutional Affairs, 2002a, website

---

In addition to the case law in relation to a patient's right to determine what happens to his or her body, there is also the influence of the Human Rights Act (UK) 1998. As discussed in *Chapter 1*, this statute incorporates into UK law the bulk of the substantive rights set out in the European Convention on Human Rights. Of particular relevance are Article 2, the *Right to Life*; Article 3, the *Prohibition of Torture, Inhuman or Degrading Treatment or Punishment;* and Article 8, the *Right to Respect for Private and Family Life*. Article 2 is what is known as a limited right where the limitations are explicitly stated in the wording of the article, Article 3 is an absolute right and Article 8 is a qualified right, where derogation is permitted but any action must be based in law, meet Convention aims, be non-discriminatory, necessary in a democratic society and proportionate (Committee on Medical Ethics, 2000). Although there was some concern that Article 2, the *Right to Life*, might prevent the forgoing of life-prolonging treatment, this has not been the case. A High Court decision involving two patients, *NHS Trust A v M; NHS Trust B v H [2001]*, taken only days after the implementation of the Human Rights Act (UK) 1998, confirmed that, where withdrawal of

> **Box 2.2 Questions for doctors to ask in order to decide whether someone has support and capacity***
>
> ■ Does the person have all the information or a sufficient amount of information needed to make the decision? If there is a choice, has any information been given on any alternatives?
> ■ Could the information be explained or presented in a way that is easier for the person to understand?
> ■ Are there particular times of day when the person's understanding is better or particular places where they may feel more at ease? Can the decision be put off until the circumstances are right for the person concerned?
> ■ Can anyone else help or support the person to make choices or express a view, such as another family member or, if appropriate, an independent advocate?
>
> * From Leaflet 2: Department of Constitutional Affairs 2002b, website

artificial nutrition and hydration were in the patients' best interests, there was no breach of Article 2. Dame Elizabeth Butler-Sloss, held that the Human Rights Act did not affect the principles laid down in the Bland case. Notwithstanding these decisions, there is no doubt that all public authorities will have to consider patients' rights very carefully when making healthcare decisions with the potential to impact upon them. The BMA Committee on Medical Ethics (2000) suggests that there are now two further questions that must always be asked:

■ Are someone's human rights affected by the decision? And, if so,
■ Is it legitimate to interfere with them?

# Capacity

Capacity and competence are terms often used interchangeably to identify the characteristics of people who are capable of making their own decisions. However, capacity seems to be the term that will be more widely used in future. The Lord Chancellor's Department's *Making Decisions* Leaflets 2 and 4 provide valuable advice on the legal concept of capacity (Department of Constitutional Affairs, 2002b, c). Leaflet 4, *The Guide for Legal Professionals* explains that 'different levels of capacity are required for different activities and the tests to determine whether a person has any particular capacity originate in law' (Department of Constitutional Affairs,

> ## Box 2.3. Questions to ask once all support and assistance has been given*
>
> ■ Is there a specific test of legal capacity for the decision in question?
> ■ Can the person meet the requirements set out in the legal test?
> ■ Does the person have a general understanding of what the decision is and why they are being asked to make it?
> ■ Does the person have a general understanding of the consequences of making, or not making, this decision?
> ■ Is the person able to understand and weigh up the information provided as part of the process of arriving at a decision?
>
> *From Leaflet 2: Department of Constitutional Affairs 2002b website

2002c). Some tests for capacity in England, such as the capacity to provide evidence in court, are set out in statute, whereas others are set out in case law, such as the capacity to make a will or drawing up an Enduring Power of Attorney document.

The law tends to regard doctors as experts in the assessment of mental capacity, but if there is a dispute about capacity, then the court will make the decision. However, it is acknowledged that there is no universally accepted definition of mental capacity because it is difficult to determine whether a decision is 'right' or 'wrong'. Similarly, even if a person is designated as having some level of mental incapacity, they may still be able to make certain decisions (Department of Constitutional Affairs, 2002b).

For legal tests of capacity, medical practitioners are referred to *Assessment of Mental Capacity: Guidance for Doctors and Lawyers* published jointly by the British Medical Association and the Law Society (2002). In the 1997 case of *Re MB (Medical treatment)* the court identified a lack of capacity has occurred when:

■ The patient is unable to understand and retain the information which is material to the decision, especially as to the likely consequences of having or not having the treatment in question; and

■ The patient is unable to use the information and weigh it in the balance as part of the process of arriving at the decision.

Leaflet 2 provides a series of questions for doctors to ask in order to decide whether someone lacks capacity. They are set out in *Box 2.2*.

Once the doctors have ensured that everything has been done to help and support the person to participate to the fullest extent possible, there is another set of key questions to ask which are set out in *Box 2.3*.

The document points out

*The doctor's role is to consider the consequences of medical conditions which may compromise an individual's ability to meet the legal requirements for capacity. If there is no medical condition, there can be no relevant medical evidence as to capacity.*

# Advance directives and proxy decision making

The discussions on patients' rights to refuse treatment and capacity lead on to the critical question of whether patients' rights to refuse treatment can be assured if they lack capacity. The solution seems to lie with the concept of 'prospective autonomy' which is 'based on the proposition that the personal values and priorities of patients ought to inform decisions about their care, even after they have lost their decisional capacity' (Rich, 2002, p.127). It is also known as 'precedent autonomy' (Dworkin, 1993) and has been argued not to be autonomy in the normal sense, but to be related to respecting decisions made while an individual is competent, even if these decisions may seem to contradict their desires when considered incompetent (Moody, 2003). They are considered to be of particular importance in the care of patients with dementia, as the prognosis of incapacity is clear from the outset of the disease, and it is thus possible actively to ascertain the patient's wishes about an almost certain future scenario (Jones, 2001; Blasi *et al*, 2002; Volicer *et al*, 2002).

## Advance directives

The idea of attempting to ascertain what the patient's wishes would be in relation to their treatment was discussed in the review of case law above, but it was the US Supreme Court in Cruzan (1990) that identified the requirement for 'clear and convincing evidence'. The Patient Self-Determination Act, with its requirements for all public facilities to provide patients with information about advance directives, was proclaimed in the same year. The information about advance directives is required to be presented on admission or before the first visit to a nursing home, and must include an explanation of the patient's right to refuse medical treatment and to execute an advance directive according to the laws of the State (Ryan, 2004).

Clearly, advance directives have been determined to be 'clear and convincing evidence' of a patient's wishes about future treatment. Their purpose is to 'allow competent individuals to inform healthcare professionals of their preferences regarding medical treatment in the event of their incapacity to communicate' (Quinlan, 2004, p.19). To date in America all 50 States and the District of Columbia have advance directive statutes (Ryan, 2004). However, recent figures suggest that fewer than 30% of all Americans have completed advance directives, with the numbers being lowest among Hispanic or Spanish speaking, those with high school education or less, those with low income and the uninsured (Kyba, 2002).

In addition, despite the fact that clinicians are concerned about providing burdensome, non-beneficial treatments to patients at the end of life, the analysis of a 12-year study demonstrates that the practices persist. Reasons for this were identified as (Solomon, 2001):

- Disseminated responsibility, wherein no single clinician is responsible for providing patients and families with an overview of the likely disease trajectory.
- Inadequate strategies for resolving tension between the need to sustain hope and optimism in patients while providing balanced, forthright guidance about possible negative outcomes and the likelihood of death.
- Reluctance to discuss quality-of-life issues with patients and families.
- Misunderstandings about what is ethically and legally possible.

The Joint Commission on Accreditation of Healthcare Organizations (JCAHO) has now identified the presence of documentation that patients have been advised about advance directives as a quality indicator. There is a positive correlation between receiving advice about an advance directive in a health maintenance organisation and deciding to complete one (Gordon and Shade, 1999).

Similar concerns about over-treatment at the end of life have been expressed in the UK by the Alzheimer's Society, which has criticised the fact that people in the terminal stages of dementia are artificially fed and hydrated (Moody, 2003). England has not legislated for advance directives to date, although the House of Lords acknowledged in Bland (1993) that an advance directive identifying a refusal of treatment had legal status, which has since been recognised by legal academics and followed by other courts (Moody, 2003). However, the British Medical Association (1995) has advised that advance authorisation of treatment carries moral, but not legal weight, and that no-one can authorise an illegal act, such as euthanasia or assisted suicide, in advance. This inability to authorise an illegal act was confirmed in *Pretty* v *Director of Public Prosecutions and Secretary of State for Home Department [2001]*, where Mrs Pretty, who was dying of motor neurone disease, petitioned the court to allow the Director of Public Prosecutions (DPP) to pardon her husband in advance for assisting her to commit suicide. The combined Full Bench of the Supreme Court of the

Queen's Bench held that the DPP had no statutory or other power to give any undertaking in relation to future or proposed criminal conduct.

The UK Nursing and Midwifery Council also recognises the status of advance directives in Section 3.6 of the Code of Professional Conduct (2002), which states

*When patients or clients are no longer legally competent and have thus lost the capacity to consent to or refuse treatment, you should try to find out whether they have previously indicated preferences in an advance statement. You must respect any refusal of treatment or care given when they were legally competent, provided the decision is clearly applicable to the present circumstances and there is no reason to believe that they have changed their minds.*

Despite these developments, Diggory and Judd (2000) conducted a study which indicated that only 50% of the 247 responding NHS trusts had taken any action about implementing advance directives, although 76% of them reported they would be in favour of national guidelines.

Having no statutory framework for advance directives means that many issues, such as duration of effect, liability for healthcare professionals, questions of what may or may not be excluded, management of relatives and drafting provisions are still left as both discretionary and optional issues. The only place for legal resolution would then be through the common law, which means that some parties will have been sufficiently dissatisfied with the clinical process of decision-making that they needed to seek resolution from the courts (Dimond, 2000). Concerns about misinterpretation (Ackroyd, 2003) and applicability to future events (Cartwright, 2000) are acknowledged as being problems with advance directives. However, it seems clear that the value of clear and convincing evidence of pre-determined wishes in relation to treatment outweighs any disadvantages. The existence of such documents may relieve both relatives and healthcare professionals of the burden of best-guessing the patient's wishes; diminish the risk of relatives imposing their own views on the decision-making process; and relieve the healthcare team of the necessity of weighing up the importance of different relatives' views (Quinlan, 2004).

Other countries, such as Australia, have legislated for advance directives in some States but not others, and the types of medical treatment that can be refused in advance varies from State to State. However, Victoria, which has the most permissive legislation in relation to what treatments might be refused and in what circumstances, reports that, because of the Medical Treatment Act 1988 (Vic) there is very little common law. The Senior Guardian of the Office of the Public Advocate believes this is because most end-of-life decisions are resolved amicably within the policy and legal framework developed by the Medical

> ## Box 2.4. Information to be contained in an advance directive*
>
> ■ List of the individual's values as a basis for others to reach appropriate decisions.
> ■ Requests for all medically reasonable efforts to be made to prolong life or express preferences between treatment options.
> ■ Where the individual wants to be cared for (eg. at home or in a specified residential facility), and/or
> ■ A waiver covering pregnancy might be written into the statement, as women of child-bearing age should be advised to consider the possibility of their advance statement being invoked at a time when they are pregnant.
>
> *From Travis et al, 2001b, p.498

Treatment Act (Carter, 2003). The New South Wales Health Department has recently introduced two advisory documents, *Using Advance Care Directives New South Wales* (New South Wales Department of Health, 2004) and *Guidelines for End-Of-Life Care and Decision-Making* (New South Wales Department of Health, 2005). Failure to comply with a properly developed advance care directive is identified in the document as potentially actionable in trespass to the person (New South Wales Department of Health, 2004, p.9)

Travis *et al* (2001b) provide useful guidance for the content of an advance directive. They suggest that the following must be included: full name; address; name and address of general practitioner; whether advice was sought from health professionals; signature of patient; date drafted and reviewed; witnessed; clear statement of the patient's wishes, either general or specific; and name, address and telephone number of patient's nominated person, if one is chosen. They suggest the information contained in *Box 2.4* also be considered for inclusion.

Travis *et al* also suggest that a member of the long-term healthcare team is well placed to witness the advance directive, as they will then have a better understanding of exactly what the patient intended (2001b). Doukas and Hardwig go further and recommend that, instead of what they describe as the 'document-based morass' (p.1155) vague statements of refusal can create, that doctors, patients and families should enter into a 'family covenant' with their own medical practitioner. They argue, 'just as informed consent is a process, not an event, the family covenant is an evolution of advance care planning beyond the execution of a document' (Doukas and Hardwig, 2003, p.1156).

Four basic elements are required to be fulfilled for an effective advance directive. They are: competency at the time of decision making; freedom from undue influence; the availability of adequate information; and clarity that the advance refusal was intended to apply to the situation that arises (Kennedy and Grubb, 2000).

## Implementation of advance directives

In terms of implementation of advance directives, the need for public education is critical. In jurisdictions where advance directives have a statutory basis, it is common to provide written advice on what the content, processes and limitations of the advance directives entail (eg. Office of the Attorney General, State of Maryland, 2003). Similarly, healthcare practitioners also require education and difficulties can arise if this is not provided. Despite established advance directive provisions in most States of Australia, there is still resistance among some health professionals to honour advance directives (Cartwright, 2000). Similarly, general practitioners (GPs) in South Australia experience ongoing difficulties in both advising patients about advance directives and actually having the discussions with them and their families, despite the fact that South Australia first introduced legislation in 1983 (Brown, 2002). Doctors have identified billing difficulties as another problem with advance directives, as the discussions are lengthy and often take up significant medical time (Brown, 2002; Doukas and Hardwig, 2003). Cultural sensitivities also need to be taken into account in developing advance directives, as not all cultures relish the notion of autonomy, valuing family decision-making during illness rather than individuality (Zimring, 2001). Storage of advance directives and the need for review also need to be discussed and determined when the process of writing the advance directive is undertaken (Travis *et al*, 2001b).

One of the major difficulties for health professionals in providing advice to patients in order for them to make an advance directive is the question of when medical treatment becomes futile. Even in America, where the courts have explored the question of futility on a number of occasions, the American Medical Association still noted in 1999 that their recommended course of action for addressing futility questions was still unclear in relation to its legal ramifications. In Texas, the Advance Directives Act 1999 has established a legally sanctioned, extra-judicial process for determining end-of-life disputes, which has led to a 67% increase in medical futility consultations and a 100% increase in right-to-die consultations in the first 12 months following the introduction of the legislation. The benefits of the changes are reported to be the conceptual and temporal boundaries that it provides for such debates. Conceptually, it encourages both families and health professionals to reconsider what is appropriate care in the circumstances and it provides a forum for debate and discussion. Temporally, the law provides for a 12-day period for resolving disputes over futile treatment (Fine and Mayo, 2003).

While some health professionals feel that the extra-judicial process takes decision making power away from the treating physician (Berger, 2004) and others believe that futility is in fact a smokescreen for simply allowing people to die (Finucane, 2004), others are supportive and see the process as a legitimate way for difficult futility decisions to be made (Fine and Mayo, 2003; Flamm and Smith, 2004). The recent case of *Hudson* v *Texas Children's Hospital [2005]* highlighted the application of a determination of futility and the concomitant decision that there was no requirement to continue futile care. In this 2005 case, the mother of a six-month old child Sun, who was ventilator dependent due to a rare lung disease called thanatophoric dysplasia, sought an order for doctors to continue treating her son against the determination of the hospital's bioethics committee, that had resolved that there was no obligation to continue Sun's treatment because it was futile. Under Texas law, Mrs Hudson then had 10 days to find another treatment facility, but the time ran out and she sought court intervention, which was denied. Citing bias due to comments of the judge, she appealed the decision and her appeal was upheld. However, on rehearing by another judge, her application was again denied based on the determination of futility and the child subsequently died (McPhee and Stewart, 2005). While this case presents a distressing picture of the mother trying to obtain a different decision about the determination of futility, it nevertheless demonstrates the application of the determination and the resolution of this difficult decision by the courts in the absence of a consensus view. However, while Mareiniss argues that futility was in fact the underlying rationale for the decision in Schiavo, he postulates that asserting that care is futile runs the risk of depriving the patient of the right to self-determination. As has already been discussed, autonomy or self-determination currently goes to the heart of the justification for refusal of treatment (2005, p.251).

### Proxy decision making

While the need for advance directives as a form of prospective autonomy seems clear, proxy decision making in end-of-life issues is less well established. The healthcare proxy is usually required to be

> *Written evidence that a patient has officially designated a family member or loved one to make medical decisions for him, should he become too incapacitated to make them himself. The agent must act in accordance with the patient's wishes and values, to the best of his ability. If the patient's wishes aren't known, it is up to the healthcare provider, in conjunction with the proxy, to act in the patient's best interest.' (Ryan, 2004, p.59)*

In America, the status given to proxy decision makers is far more limited than that given to the status of the patient through advance directives. For example, New York requires 'clear and convincing evidence' of the patient's wishes, which probably means that only a comprehensive written advance directive would suffice. Twelve other States permit proxies to make decisions about artificial nutrition only if they have been specifically authorised to do so by the patient. In another seven States the ability of a proxy to decide must be specifically authorised by the patient and in 37 States there is a hierarchy of people named who might act as proxy, but their scope of decision making is severely restricted (Gillick, 2004).

When a person's wishes are not known, the English courts have determined that the decision ought to be made in the 'best interests' of the individual, and the factors determining best interests were laid out earlier in this chapter (Department for Constitutional Affairs, 2002a). One of the difficulties in determining 'best interests' is the fact that families may not always be unanimous in their views of what is right for their loved one, and in such cases the courts may be called in to intervene. Certainly in America, when the courts have been called in to determine the patient's best interests in cases of last resort, they have traditionally erred 'on the side of life' and have opted for life-prolonging treatment on most occasions (Rich, 2002, p.128). However, this was not the case in the recent Schiavo decision where, despite significant family dispute about the best interests of the patient, the courts consistently and repeatedly authorised withdrawal of nutrition and hydration.

## Conclusion

This is the first of two chapters examining legal and ethical issues in end-of-life care. This chapter has looked particularly at the notion of personhood in end-of-life care, focusing on the patient's right to decide what happens to his or her body, and particularly the right to refuse treatment. It has also examined what happens if the patient is unable to refuse treatment due to incapacity, both when the patient's wishes as to treatment are known and when they are not. *Chapter 3* examines therapeutic issues arising in end-of-life care, including the use of opiates and the consequences of refusal of treatment on clinical care.

# CHAPTER 3

# Legal and ethical issues: Clinical practice

This chapter builds on the discussions on personhood in *Chapter 2* and examines the clinical issues surrounding end-of-life care, including the therapeutic issues around opiate administration such as the doctrine of double effect, issues arising from a patient's right to refuse treatment, such as forgoing life-sustaining medical treatment, decisions not to attempt resuscitation and more controversial issues such as assistance in dying, physician-assisted suicide and euthanasia.

## The doctrine of double effect

This concept has been described as 'a doctrine that distinguishes between the consequences a person intends and those that are unintended but foreseen and may be applicable in various situations where an action has two effects, one good and one bad' (Williams, 2001, p.41). It has its origins in mediaeval times and has been applied particularly in recent years to questions related to providing pain relief in end-of-life care, where health professionals have been concerned or even aware that the large doses of pain relief, which were to be administered, would concomitantly shorten the patient's life (Ford, 2002; Jolly and Cornock, 2003). It is known that nurses (Volker, 2001) and doctors (Shah and Lloyd-Williams, 2003) confuse administration of adequate pain relief with physician-assisted suicide (PAS), aid in dying (AID) and euthanasia. One of the seven legal myths identified as barriers to end-of-life care by the 1997 Consensus Panel of the American College of Physicians and the American College of Internal Medicine was that 'if a physician prescribes or administers high doses of medication to relieve pain or other discomfort in a terminally ill patient, resulting in death, he/she will be criminally prosecuted' (Meisel *et al*, 2000, p.2497). Shah and Lloyd-Williams (2003) go so far as to suggest that health professionals suffer from 'opioid phobia'. This is borne out by the WHO policy documents on cancer pain discussed in *Chapter 1*, which have as a key strategy the need to educate healthcare professionals about the need for adequate pain relief and to de bunk some of the myths around pain management in palliative care (WHO, 1990, 1996, 2000).

However, giving opiates with the intention of relieving pain is ethically, legally and medically acceptable, even if the doses are exceptionally high, provided that the intent is to relieve pain, and even if the dose may shorten the patient's life (Australian Medical Association, 1997; Kyba, 2002; Jolly and Cornock, 2003). Four criteria have been identified to meet the doctrine of double effect.

> *First, the action must be morally good or at least indifferent. This requires some evaluation of the moral standing of the action to be made, independent of its intended outcome. Second, the good effect must be intended, even if the secondary effect is foreseen ...Third, the good effect must not be achieved by way of the bad, otherwise it would be using a bad means to a good end. Finally, the good result must outweigh the bad result. This requires a judgement. (Jolly and Cornock, 2003, p.240)*

Health professionals working in palliative and end-of-life care are usually more comfortable with giving adequate pain relief than those working in acute care. A study interviewing nurses working mainly in palliative and end-of-life care who had received requests for assistance in dying (AID) demonstrated that they were morally able to distinguish between 'opiate-related hastened death' and 'opiate-related caused death'. They accepted the inevitability of 'opiate-related hastened death' because they believed that effective pain management was a moral imperative for their dying patients (Schwarz, 2003). However, it is clear that, despite the advice of the WHO, confusion still persists in relation to this topic. It will be seen that this becomes particularly problematic in the debates over PAS, AID and euthanasia.

## Do-not-attempt-resuscitation (DNAR) orders

The outcome of do-not-attempt-resuscitation (DNAR) orders, previously known as do-not-resuscitate (DNR) or not-for-resuscitation (NFR) orders, has been to deliberately withhold resuscitation measures, most usually cardio-pulmonary resuscitation (CPR) from a person when he or she has undergone a cardiac arrest. It first arose in cardiac theatres when the heart stopped during cardiac surgery (Costello, 2002) and was often undertaken internally in those circumstances. CPR was intended for victims of cardiac or respiratory arrest who had good survival prognoses (Kyba, 2002) but by the late 1960s CPR had become the 'poster child of the era of miracles in medicine' (Lynn and Gregory, 2003). By the mid-1970s and until the present day, CPR has been available to all patients, including those with serious chronic illness, unless a DNAR order has been implemented (Kyba, 2002; Lynn and Gregory, 2003).

However, CPR is only effective in certain groups of patients, and the elderly do not usually have good prognoses. CPR as a life-saving procedure has (not surprisingly) been described as futile for most palliative care patients, and discussion about CPR is usually sufficient to decrease requests for it in this group (Costello, 2002). Much of the literature has explored 'the right to forgo' CPR, but Lynn and Gregory (2003) suggest that it would be better to describe 'the folly of applying desperate measures to patients whose lives were nearly spent, even if the resuscitation would restore circulation for a short time' (p.1502). Certainly, one recent study reveals the number of patients surviving to discharge following CPR ranges from only 6.5% to 15% (Leonard *et al*, 1999).

It has been suggested that there is a need to obtain patient consent to write a DNAR order and this would certainly seem to be in accord with the need to discuss futile treatment with patients (Biegler, 2003). But a genuine concern is that a DNAR discussion or order has become a metaphor for a full discussion about end-of-life care (Lynn and Gregory, 2003), if indeed any discussion occurs about the DNAR order at all. A study on elderly patients in the North of England revealed that, of the 56 patients who formed the backdrop for a study of doctors' and nurses' attitudes about DNAR orders, there was no evidence to suggest that any of them had ever been involved in their own DNAR orders, despite the trust policy stipulating the need for involvement (Costello, 2002). One New Zealand hospital has developed two policies, one for when patients request DNAR and one for when medical staff feel it is appropriate. Both policies require a form to be filled in which contains the signatures of the medical staff, nurses, patients and, where appropriate, relatives (Paterson, 2000).

Difficulties such as those identified above, plus the introduction of the Human Rights Act (UK) 1998, indicated to the British Medical Association (BMA) the need for guidelines on decisions relating to cardiopulmonary resuscitation. In 2001 the BMA issued a Joint Statement with the UK Resuscitation Council and the Royal College of Nursing entitled *Decisions Relating to Cardiopulmonary Resuscitation*, which recommended that all establishments should have local policies in place for decision making if they are likely to face decisions about attempting resuscitation. The purpose of the guidelines is 'to outline the legal and ethical standards for planning patient care and decision making in relation to CPR' and the focus of the guidelines is 'situations in which decisions are made in advance and form part of the patient's care plan'. Emergency situations where no advance decision has been made are also covered.

A summary of the joint statement is reproduced in full in *Box 3.1* because it provides an excellent overview of this important document.

This document is an extremely valuable contribution to the DNAR debate and sets some clear guidelines for healthcare professionals and provides some realistic expectations for patients and their families. However, not all the issues identified in this document are completely resolved at this time. For example, the guidelines make it clear that responsibility for DNAR decisions rests with the

**Box 3.1. Summary of decisions relating to
cardio-pulmonary resuscitation\***

*Principles*

■ Timely support for patients and people close to them, and effective, sensitive communication are essential.

■ Decisions must be based on the individual's circumstances and must be reviewed regularly.

■ Sensitive advance discussion should always be encouraged but not forced.

■ Information about CPR and the chances of a successful outcome need to be realistic.

*Practical matters*

■ Information about CPR policies should be displayed for patients and staff.

■ Leaflets should be available for patients and people close to them explaining about CPR, how decisions are made and their involvement in decisions.

■ Decisions about attempting CPR must be communicated effectively to relevant health professionals.

*In emergencies*

■ If no advance decision has been made or is known, CPR should be attempted unless:
> the patient has refused CPR
> the patient is clearly in the terminal phase of illness, or
> the burdens of the treatment outweigh the benefits.

*Advance decision making*

■ Competent patients should be involved in discussions about attempting CPR unless they indicate that they do not want to be.

■ Where patients lack competence to participate, people close to them can be helpful in reflecting their views.

*Legal issues*

■ Patients' rights under the Human Rights Act must be taken into account in decision making.

■ Neither patients nor relatives can demand treatment which the healthcare team judges to be inappropriate, but all efforts will be made to accommodate wishes and preferences.

■ In England, Wales and Northern Ireland relatives and people close to the patient are not entitled in law to take healthcare decisions for the patient.

■ In Scotland, adults may appoint a healthcare proxy to give consent for medical treatment.

■ Health professionals need to be aware of the law in relation to decision making for children and young people.

\*From British Medical Association et al, 2001, p.17

patient's GP or consultant. Despite the fact the Royal College of Nursing was a signatory to the document, there have been calls for greater nurse involvement in DNAR decisions (Castledine, 2004) and recently, a hospital's alleged 'unlawful refusal' to resuscitate a disabled 10-year-old girl with breathing difficulties was challenged in the High Court after the nurses took matters into their own hands, resuscitated the child and put her on an adult ventilator (Dyer, 2004a). Other questions still being asked are how to communicate DNAR decisions to potential resuscitators when people are in the community (Michael, 2002; Lynn and Gregory, 2003) and whether patients who have surgery ought to have DNAR orders suspended while in the operating theatre (Goldberg, 2002).

## Forgoing life-prolonging or life-sustaining treatment

The term 'forgoing' is used here to incorporate both withholding and withdrawing life-sustaining medical treatment. Despite the fact that differentiation is often made between the two from an emotional perspective (Paterson, 2000; Seymour *et al*, 2000) there is strong legal, professional and ethical opinion that there is no difference (Hastings Center, 1987; Stanley, 1992; American Academy of Paediatrics, 1994; British Medical Association, 2001; UK General Medical Council, 2002; Scanlon, 2003). Similarly, the terms life-sustaining medical treatment and life-prolonging medical treatment seem to be used interchangeably, but for the purpose of this chapter the term life-sustaining medical treatment (LSMT) will be used to represent both.

Within the literature LSMT is differentiated from nursing care, which is described by the General Medical Council (2002), in the absence of a legal definition, as

*... procedures or medications which are solely or primarily aimed at providing comfort to a patient or alleviating that person's pain, symptoms or distress. It includes the offer of oral nutrition and hydration.*

The critical aspect of LSMT is that it refers to medical treatment, not nursing care as defined above. LSMT includes CPR, artificial ventilation, use of antibiotics and renal dialysis, and artificial nutrition and hydration (Cartwright, 2000). Artificial nutrition and hydration is further defined as,

*Techniques such as the use of nasogastric tubes, percutaneous endoscopic gastrostomy (gastric PEG), subcutaneous hydration, or intravenous cannula, to provide a patient with nutrition and hydration where a patient has a problem taking fluids or food orally. A distinction is usually made between such artificial means and oral nutrition and hydration where food or drink is given by mouth, the latter being regarded as part of nursing care. (General Medical Council, 2002)*

However, certain medical treatments can also legitimately form part of palliative care, for example, blood transfusions, intravenous fluids, treating hypercalcaemia, and even the use of antibiotics and stents, but their purpose would only be to relieve distressing symptoms (Shah and Lloyd-Williams, 2003). Shah and Lloyd-Williams (2003) further make the point that, in terminal care 'no treatment is undertaken merely with a view to prolong life, and no treatment is withheld or withdrawn to hasten death' (p.213).

Article 2 of the Human Rights Act 1998, which incorporates the provisions of the European Convention on Human Rights, identifies a right to life. However, in *A NHS Trust* v *D & Ors [2000]*, a case concerning a decision not to resuscitate a severely disabled 19-month-old child with a very short life expectancy, Cazalet J made it clear that Article 2 does not require the prolongation of life in all circumstances. This interpretation of Article 2 was confirmed in *NHS Trust A* v *M: NHS Trust B* v *H [2001]* where it was confirmed that non-treatment was in the best interests of two patients in PVS.

The two key factors that will determine whether a treatment can be forgone are firstly, the patient's right to refuse a treatment and secondly, whether it is in the patient's 'best interests' to forgo the treatment. In Chapter 2 the patient's right to refuse treatment was identified as being legal and not the same as suicide, even if that refusal meant ultimately that the patient would die. For example, in *Re Conroy [1985]*, the New Jersey Supreme Court held that:

*Declining life-sustaining treatment may not properly be viewed as an attempt to commit suicide. Refusing medical treatment merely allows the disease to take its natural course; if death were eventually to occur, it would be the result, primarily, of the underlying disease and not the result of a self-inflicted injury.*

Similarly in *Re C [1994]*, a patient at Broadmoor refused to have a leg amputated 'on the grounds that he would prefer to die with two legs than survive with one'. He sought an injunction from the court not to allow the doctors to remove his leg without his permission. The court held that, provided he understood the nature and the consequences of his decision and had the mental capacity to make the decision, it was his to make and his decision was binding on the doctors.

If the patient does not have capacity to refuse treatment at the time that treatment is offered, then the question of proxy decision making arises. To ascertain the patient's wishes, there is still the need for 'clear and convincing evidence' of those wishes, such as an advance directive. In the absence of such evidence, the decision makers are expected to act in the patient's 'best interests', as previously discussed in Bland (1993).

In deciding whether or not it is in the patients 'best interests' to forgo the treatment, Glare and Tobin (2002) offer three other criteria in addition to refusal by the patient. They state that LSMT may legitimately be forgone if it is: therapeutically futile; overly burdensome to the patient; and/or not reasonably available without disproportionate hardship to the patient's carers or others.

Although the use of the term 'futile' is not without its critics (Luce and Alpers, 2001), it is used quite regularly within the literature on LSMT and is thus worthy of exploration. The argument used is that if a treatment 'could make no significant contribution to the patient's cure or improvement, nor sustain the patient in a tolerable condition' (Glare and Tobin, 2002, p.81) then it would be therapeutically futile and could be forgone. Luce and Alpers (2001, p.41) distinguish between therapeutic or physiologic futility and medical futility. Physiologic futility is where 'if treatment cannot achieve its intended purpose, then to withhold it does not cause harm', whereas they clearly have concerns that medical futility is more value-laden and subjective, based on the physician's decision as to whether a treatment is going to do anything more than maintain the status quo. Notwithstanding this critique, there is acknowledgement within the English guidance documents that some value judgement will have to be made by the doctor, most desirably with good family and carer involvement. For example, the General Medical Council (2002) advises

*Not continuing or not starting a potentially life-prolonging treatment is in the best interests of a patient when it would provide no net benefit to the patient ...Where a patient's wishes are not known it is the doctor's responsibility to decide what is in the patient's best interests. However, this cannot be done effectively without information which (sic) those close to the patient will be best placed to know.*

Similarly the Lord Chancellor's Office recommends checking with a number of people, the patient's GP, family, friends and other health professionals, to try to determine what is in the patient's best interests (Department for Constitutional Affairs, 2002b). Where there is indecision or disagreement as to whether or not a treatment is likely to be of no therapeutic benefit, it is suggested that a trial of the treatment be carried out, with clear parameters for discontinuation agreed in advance (General Medical Council, 2002; Scanlon, 2003). If agreement still cannot be reached, it is recognised that there will be the need for recourse to the courts (British Medical Association, 2001; Department for Constitutional Affairs, 2002b; General Medical Council, 2002). In America, where the courts have been asked to make an advance decision about forgoing LSMT, they have usually 'erred on the side of life'. It has been noted that 'physicians are likely to get better legal results when they refuse to provide non-beneficial treatment and then defend their decisions in court as consistent with professional standards than when they seek advance permission from a court to withhold care' (Luce and Alpers, 2001, p.42).

Potentially it could be problematic always to emphasise the primacy of the doctor as taking clinical responsibility for decision making, even a junior doctor in some situations (General Medical Council, 2002). However, with increasing emphasis on clinical career paths for highly experienced specialist nurses, there will be nurses practising in clinical areas who will have greater knowledge and expertise than junior doctors and as much relevant specialist clinical knowledge and expertise as their medical counterparts. In the majority of cases, all clinicians will agree on what constitutes the best interests of the patient, but future documents need to acknowledge that there will be situations where a nurse might be the most experienced and knowledgeable specialist clinician to make the decision.

Potential and actual patients have also challenged the primacy of the doctor. In *Glass* v *United Kingdom [2004]* a mother applied on behalf of her severely mentally and physically handicapped son to the European Court of Human Rights, and won a declaration that 'the decision of the authorities to override the second applicant's [mother's] objection to the proposed treatment [injections of diamorphine] in the absence of authorisation by a court resulted in a breach of Article 8 of the [European] Convention [on Human Rights]'. The applicants were awarded €10000 in damages. The Court recognised that the doctors believed they were acting, in their clinical judgement, in the patient's best interests. However, it determined that, given the deadlock between the mother and the doctors over the proposed course of treatment (palliative care), a court ruling should have been sought and it was this failure to do so which caused the breach of Article 8. A similar case, *Portsmouth NHS Trust* v *Wyatt [2004]*, concerning a severely mentally and physically disabled 11-month-old girl, Charlotte Wyatt, was decided by the High Court in 2004 (Frith, 2004a). The doctors believed that she should not be resuscitated if she stopped breathing again because to ventilate her would 'be futile and even cruel', particularly as she has only a 1% chance of surviving for another year. However, the parents, who attribute their desire for resuscitation to their Christian beliefs, wanted the doctors not only to ventilate the infant, but also to give her a tracheostomy, because they wished to spend more time with her. Hedley J applied three principles, the sanctity of life, the best interests of the child and the inherent right of the child to respect for her dignity. In a moving judgment, he determined that 'any further aggressive treatment, even if necessary to prolong life, is not in her [Charlotte's] best interests'. He based his decision on three answers to his question, 'What can be done to benefit Charlotte?' The answers were:

- First, that she can be given as much comfort and as little pain as possible;
- Second, that she can be given as much time as possible to spend physically in the presence of and in contact with her parents; and
- Third, that she can meet her end whenever that may be in what Mr Wyatt calls the TLC of those who love her most. (*Portsmouth NHS Trust* v *Wyatt [2004]*)

In April 2005, Hedley J was again called to rule on a further determination in relation to Charlotte Wyatt. In *Wyatt* v *Portsmouth NHS Trust [2005]*, the parties returned before the courts to seek the judge's determination of two questions in the light of the best interests test. Charlotte had survived the winter and was in fact in a much improved respiratory condition than she had been at the time of Hedley J's previous determination in October 2004. Notwithstanding her improved respiratory status, she was still considered to be terminally ill, was losing weight, despite excellent physical care, due to her constant vomiting and excessive involuntary movements, and had experienced no brain growth, having still the brain of the size of a newborn baby.

The two questions Hedley J was called to determine were firstly, whether or not, in the event of the agreed inevitable 'respiratory crisis', Charlotte should be transferred to a tertiary centre and intensive care unit and ventilated. Secondly, if the decision was that such invasive treatment should be withheld, should such a decision be made at the time of the hearing or at the time of the event of the respiratory crisis? Hedley J, after hearing extensive medical evidence, held that it would not be in Charlotte's best interests 'to die in the course of futile aggressive treatment' (at para 17). He also determined that, in the light of the ongoing differences of opinion between the family and the hospital in relation to Charlotte's ongoing treatment in the light of a respiratory crisis, that the decision should be taken at the time of the hearing and not left until a crisis eventuated.

A second similar case, that of Luke Winston-Jones, who had Edwards syndrome, a rare genetic disorder that causes severe physical and mental developmental problems, was decided before the High Court on Friday 22 October 2004. (Frith, 2004b). Dame Elizabeth Butler-Sloss, in the Family Division of the High Court, affirmed Hedley J's October statement of the law relating to best interests in *Re L (A child) [2004]* and gave Royal Liverpool Children's NHS Trust and North West Wales NHS Trust permission to withhold mechanical ventilation should Luke's condition worsen (UK Clinical Ethics Network, 2004).

In addition to these cases, there is also a challenge in place in relation to a hypothetical future medical decision. The advice from the General Medical Council on forgoing artificial nutrition and hydration contained in their guidance *Withholding and Withdrawing Life-Prolonging Treatments: Good*

*Practice in Decision Making* (2002) was challenged following a petition to the High Court by a man suffering from cerebellar ataxia, a degenerative brain condition. Mr Burke believed that the level of decision making power accorded to doctors under the guidelines could breach his human rights (Dyer, 2004b). Mumby J in the High Court determined that

> *The legal content of the guidance was vulnerable in four respects: in the emphasis on the right of the competent patient to refuse, rather than to require treatment; in its lack of emphasis on the duty of a doctor who is unwilling or unable to carry out a patient's wishes to continue providing treatment until he can find another doctor to take over the case; the failure to acknowledge the heavy presumption in favour of LSMT and to recognise the 'touchstone of best interests in intolerability'; and finally, the failure of the guidance to spell out the requirement to obtain judicial sanction prior to forgoing artificial nutrition and hydration.*

Mumby J held that Mr Burke had established his right to relief (*Burke* v *General Medical Council [2004]*). The General Medical Council has been given leave to appeal the decision (Dyer, 2004c). The appeal hearing commenced on 16 May 2005 and a decision has not been handed down at the time of writing.

The concept of 'overly burdensome treatment' is usually a matter of clinical judgement in weighing up the potential for improvement or maintenance of health and the relief of discomfort against the foreseeable burdens, eg. pain, discomfort, nausea, vomiting, loss of consciousness or deformity. Consultation with a palliative care team, as well as the family and current healthcare team, is proposed to assist in this judgement (Glare and Tobin, 2002). It has been suggested that inflicting overly burdensome treatment on a patient may be in breach of Article 3 under the Human Rights Act 1998, the right not to be subject to torture or inhuman or degrading treatment (British Medical Association, 2000).

In terms of what treatments may be thought to be overly burdensome, a distinction has been made between artificial nutrition and hydration and other LSMTs both in the UK (British Medical Association *et al*, 2003; General Medical Council, 2002) and in some States of America (Nolde, 2003/04). This is despite the fact that it is acknowledged that the decision to withdraw artificial ventilation usually precipitates death much faster than forgoing artificial nutrition and hydration, and the proximity between the decision and the outcome can be distressing for all involved (Scanlon, 2003). Although it is clear that forgoing artificial nutrition and hydration seems to create greater concern and anxiety with both healthcare professionals and the public (Kyba, 2002; Scanlon, 2003), there is concern that such differentiation could create further problems by creating special status for artificial nutrition and hydration as a treatment choice (Nolde, 2003/04). Legally, artificial nutrition and hydration has been identified as a medical treatment in the UK in *NHS Trust A* v *M: NHS Trust B* v *H [2001]* and in the Victorian case of *Gardner: Re BWV [2003]*. However, where artificial nutrition and hydration are to be forgone, in all cases a second opinion must be sought, and if the patient is in a PVS, currently in England, Northern Ireland and Wales, it is necessary to approach the courts for a ruling (General Medical Council, 2002).

Clinically, the provision of artificial nutrition and hydration has been argued to be contraindicated in end-of-life care. Food and fluids are unable to be processed as readily in a dying patient, and overload could lead to pulmonary congestion, peripheral oedema, ascites and even hydrocephalus; and each skin site of insertion has the potential for infection. Furthermore, problems of fluid retention could then lead to insertion of a urinary catheter, with the concomitant risk of bladder infection (Nolde, 2003/04). A series of studies has noted the benefits of terminal dehydration in imminently dying people, who, it is reported, do not suffer from hunger or thirst (Kyba, 2002).

## Physician-assisted suicide, aid-in-dying and euthanasia

These three issues, PAS, AID and euthanasia, have been grouped together because they are identified in the literature as proactive acts undertaken by physicians or others with the intent of actively hastening the patient's death (Cartwright, 2000; Kyba, 2002). In a colloquium in Amsterdam in 1999, it was agreed that the word euthanasia should only refer to giving a patient drugs intended to cause the death of a patient (eg. a lethal injection) (Colloquium of the Royal Netherlands Academy of Arts and Sciences, 1999). By contrast, in assisted suicide, where the patient is the agent, the role of the physician is to provide the medications, but not to administer them (Kyba, 2002). Assistance or aid in dying (AID) is often the overarching term to describe assisted suicide where someone else assists a person to take hir or her own life. PAS refers to where that assistance is provided by a doctor.

While euthanasia was legalised in the Northern Territory of Australia under the Rights of the Terminally Ill Act 1995 (NT), the Australian Federal Government overturned that statute in 1997 (Mendelson, 1999). However, PAS has now been legalised in Oregon under the Oregon Death with Dignity Act 1997, although the US Supreme Court made it clear in *Washington* v *Glucksberg [1997]* and *Vacco* v *Quill [1997]* that there is no constitutionally protected right to PAS. Similarly, *Pretty* v *Director of Public Prosecutions and Secretary of State for Home Department [2001]* established that there was no right to die under the Human Rights Act 1998 (UK). While Oregon is clearly increasing the potential for active intervention at end of life, other US States have been tightening up their legal framework to prevent PAS or AID. For example, the

Ohio House of Representatives has passed a Bill (HB 474) authorising State professional boards to discipline healthcare providers who assist in suicide (International Taskforce on Euthanasia and Assisted Suicide, 2002).

In contrast, The Netherlands have now legalised both voluntary euthanasia and PAS and Belgium has legalised voluntary euthanasia but not PAS (International Taskforce on Euthanasia and Assisted Suicide, 2002). Switzerland has a different legal system again, where voluntary euthanasia is illegal, but AID, providing it is for honourable and not self-serving motives, can be undertaken by any member of society, and is not the exclusive reserve of doctors (House of Lords Select Committee, 2005). Developments in The Netherlands and their effect on end-of-life care will be discussed further in Chapter 5.

The debate on euthanasia, AID and PAS can be extremely polarised. Many professional organisations, while supporting forgoing LSMT, make their opposition to PAS and euthanasia very clear (eg. Australian Medical Association, 1997; British Medical Association, 1998; Quill and Byock, 2000; Royal College of Nursing in Hemmings, 2003). However, some critics of these unequivocal positions argue that they do not reflect the reality of the debate in health professional circles and call for 'studied neutrality' in the position statements (Quill and Cassel, 2003). It is argued that banning PAS has several potential adverse consequences:

- It increases patients' fears about physicians' abandonment in the face of severe suffering.
- It reinforces physicians' tendencies not to acknowledge the intolerable suffering that some patients experience despite excellent palliative care.
- It suggests falsely bright lines between PAS and other currently available end-of-life practices that do not resonate with the beliefs of many patients, families and clinicians.
- It may explain some of the variability in access to other last-resort practices.
- It may teach patients to be less than forthright with their physicians if they desire a hastened death. (Quill and Cassel, 2003, p.208)

The arguments against both euthanasia and PAS often are of a religious nature, based on the sanctity of life (Schwarz, 2003). Others express concern about the 'slippery slope', ie. that sanctioning voluntary euthanasia may by the start of a more sinister campaign of involuntary euthanasia (Neeley, 1994). There is also concern that women might be more targeted than men in PAS and euthanasia as they are more compliant and more 'other' focused (Kohm and Brigner, 1998; Allen, 2002). Furthermore, opponents argue that if adequate pain relief is provided, there is no necessity for PAS or euthanasia (Kyba, 2002). It has even been suggested that to legalise PAS and euthanasia would result in a 'can of worms' for lawyers and bureaucrats (Cartwright, 2000). There is no doubt that the checks and balances in place in the Northern Territory legislation rendered the process extremely tortuous (Chiarella, 1995b).

However, there is also considerable support for euthanasia and PAS. Proponents argue that pain is rarely the reason that people seek these solutions. It is more likely to be shortness of breath, weakness, nausea, vomiting and open wounds (Quill and Cassel, 2003) and fear of undignified and senselessly prolonged deaths (Schwarz, 1999). It is also clear that, even with the best pain relief, some terminally ill patients still suffer (Volker, 2001). Others argue that PAS and euthanasia are already happening, so ought to be controlled (Hemmings, 2003). Furthermore, it is argued that the Oregon experience demonstrates there is no 'slippery slope' (Miller, 2000; Putnam, 2001) since three years out from the enactment of the Oregon legislation, only 0.1% of deaths were due to PAS. Contrary to the fears about targeting minority, oppressed or disadvantaged groups, of the 70 deaths, 68 were white, only one lacked insurance, only one was partly motivated by financial concerns and all had serious progressive illnesses (Quill and Cassel, 2003). What is obvious is that this is an extremely contentious area with little hope of clear-cut resolution. However, the debate has not gone away and if anything, the Oregon experience has opened the door for further developments.

The debate in England was rekindled in 2003 with the introduction of a Private Members Bill into the House of Lords by Lord Joel Joffe, a retired human rights lawyer, on 20 February 2003 (second reading 6 June 2003). The Bill, originally titled the Patient (Assisted Dying) Bill, had as its long title:

*A Bill to enable a competent adult who is suffering unbearably as a result of a terminal or a serious and progressive physical illness to receive medical help to die at his own considered and persistent request; and to make provision for a person suffering from such a condition to receive pain relief medication.*

The Bill required the person making the complaint to have his or her condition and competence verified by two doctors, an attending (regular) doctor and a consulting doctor, and to then make a declaration witnessed by a solicitor, stipulating that none of the above could benefit from the death.

The Bill was welcomed by right-to-die groups such as the Voluntary Euthanasia Society (BBC News, 20 February 2003) and the World Federation of Right-to-Die Societies (2003). However, it was strongly opposed by religious groups, the Chief Rabbi making his objections known on Jewish. com.uk (2003) and the Christian Medical Fellowship making their views known through their organisation Triple Helix (Saunders, 2003). The Royal College of Physicians (RCP) recognised that the Bill was introduced with good motivations and described it as 'a deeply human response' to the fact that, 'even in affluent societies with well-developed health services, there is much unalleviated suffering associated with illness which is in many cases incurable and sometimes terminal'. However, the RCP's submission argued that it was 'the wrong response and potentially dangerous'. It was also described as 'untimely, given the current inadequate development of first-rate palliative care services' (Royal College of Physicians Committee on Ethical Issues, 2003). The Disability Rights Commission (DRC) was also strongly opposed to the Bill, although it stated that it took very seriously 'the principle of autonomy expressed in the phrase a "right to die"'. This was clearly the wish of both Dianne Pretty, whose case was discussed earlier, and Reginald Crew, a man also suffering from motor neurone disease who obtained assistance in dying in Switzerland following the Queens Bench judgment on Mrs Pretty. The DRC expressed the view that 'alongside the voices of Reginald Crew and Dianne Pretty, we hear the voices of disabled people who express a real fear that their lives will be put at risk if voluntary euthanasia or assisted suicide were legalised' (Disability Rights Commission, 2004).

Following the level of criticism expressed by such key groups, the Bill was amended and reintroduced as the Assisted Dying for the Terminally Ill Bill 2004. Whereas the 2003 Bill was unanimously rejected by the RCP's Committee on Ethical Issues in Medicine, the RCP, in conjunction with the Academy of Medical Royal Colleges, reconsidered the amended Bill, which had addressed some of the RCP's concerns, and determined that it neither rejected nor supported the Bill, due to the 'clear division of views as to its desirability from an ethical point of view'. On this second occasion of considering the amended Bill, there was unanimous agreement that 'the Bill was a matter for society as a whole to decide and that the College should not assume a position for or against' (Academy of Medical Royal Colleges, 2004). What the Academy of Medical Royal Colleges chose to do on this occasion was to highlight those aspects of the Bill on which they believed as clinicians it was appropriate for them to comment. These included diagnosis, training, implementation, audit and documentation and campaigning for palliative care services.

The National Council for Hospice and Specialist Palliative Care Services (NCHSPCS – more simply re-named the National Council for Palliative Care in 2004), an 'umbrella organisation for palliative care in England, Wales and Northern Ireland', also chose not to make comment on whether or not physician-assisted dying (PAD) ought to be legalised in the UK in the future, but instead sought to comment on 'areas which must be researched and clarified before any decision to legalise PAD can be made; and practical issues raised by the current Bill' (NCHSPCS, 2004). Their recommendations for research will be discussed in *Chapter 6*.

Although the Chair of the Royal College of Nursing's (RCN) ethics committee spoke out personally in favour of the original Bill in 2003 (50plushealth, 2003), the Royal College of Nursing has recently confirmed its

> **Box 3.2. Recommendations of the House of Lords Select Committee First Report on the Assisted Dying for the Terminally Ill Bill**
>
> ■ An early opportunity should be taken in the next session of Parliament for a debate on our report.
> ■ If in the wake of such a debate a new Bill should be introduced by a member of the House, this should be referred, following a formal Second Reading, to a Committee of the whole House for detailed examination in the light of our report.

opposition even to the amended Bill, with the RCN General Secretary Beverley Malone stating that 'anything jeopardising the trust [in the nurse–patient relationship] could have potentially disastrous consequences for nursing, our patients and their families' (RCN, 2004).

The Bill went before a House of Lords Select Committee, which called for written submissions (including those from the NCHSPCS, RCN and Academy of Medical Royal Colleges) and held oral hearings (UK Parliament, 2004). The House of Lords Assisted Dying for the Terminally Ill Bill – First Report was published on 3 March 2005. The Select Committee not only took submissions and conducted hearings, they also visited Oregon, The Netherlands and Switzerland to learn first hand the impact of both voluntary euthanasia and assistance in dying, whether physician or lay assisted. The extent of the Committee's work was such that Lord Joffe's Bill was precluded from making progress in the session of Parliament in place in March due to shortage of time. The recommendations from the report in relation to procedural considerations for the Bill to progress are set out in *Box 3.2.*

The House of Lords Select Committee also identified a number of key issues that emerged for them during their investigations and hearings, and they strongly recommended that these be taken into account when framing up any new legislation. These included, firstly, a belief that

*The demand for assisted suicide or voluntary euthanasia is particularly strong among determined individuals whose suffering derives more from the fact of their terminal illness than from its symptoms and who are unlikely to be deflected from their wish to end their lives by more or better palliative care (House of Lords Select Committee, 2005, abstract).*

They recommended that in any new relevant legislation, consideration should be given to focusing primarily on this group of people. Secondly, they identified a strong link between the actual scope of any legislation and the number of terminally ill people who might take up the opportunity. The

Committee recommended that any new bill should distinguish clearly between assisted suicide and voluntary euthanasia, as the take-up rate is 'dramatically less' where legislation is limited to assisted suicide than in places where voluntary euthanasia is also legalised. Thirdly, the Select Committee recommended that any future bill needed to be explicit about the acts a doctor might be authorised to perform in order to effect assistance in suicide or voluntary euthanasia (eg. writing a prescription, giving a medicine, giving an injection, and what sorts of medications can actually be prescribed).

A fourth recommendation was that any future bill should take into account the clinical realities inherent in implementing some of the safeguards included in the legislation. Examples given included the difficulty of making a prognosis of the length of a terminal illness; a comprehensive understanding of the elements of an assessment of mental competence; and a recommendation to include a test for unrelievable suffering, rather than unbearable suffering or distress. Finally, the Select Committee recommended that if any future bill were to claim that palliative care was an acceptable alternative to assisted suicide or voluntary euthanasia, it was essential to ensure that such care was immediately and reliably available to all patients. This rather cryptic final recommendation highlights the fact that, even in developed countries such as England and Wales, the rhetoric of universally available palliative and end-of-life care may not match the reality.

## Conclusion

The previous two chapters have explored the legal and ethical framework in which the end-of-life care debate and relevant policy development is situated. This chapter has provided an appraisal of the key issues that have been the subject of judicial review or legislation over the past 30 years. In particular it has examined the doctrine of double effect, forgoing life-sustaining medical treatment (including artificial nutrition and hydration), do-not-attempt resuscitation orders, physician-assisted suicide, aid in dying and euthanasia. Finally, it has considered in some detail the report on a Bill to legalise physician-assisted dying in the UK, which has recently been published by a House of Lords Select Committee.

CHAPTER 4

# Policy issues relating to clinical practice developments

## Introduction

This chapter examines policy issues that impact clinical practice development. The purpose of the chapter is to examine how policy influences clinical practice and which aspects of policy ought to be the focus of attention for clinicians, rather than to review the vast array of literature about clinical practice in palliative and end-of-life care. All of the legal and ethical issues discussed in *Chapters 2 and 3* have a significant impact on clinical practice, but will only be raised again in this chapter if they are central to other issues. The policy issues that will be explored in this chapter in relation to end-of-life care are: funding; eligibility criteria; location; staffing requirements; clinical frameworks and models of care; and communication models and requirements.

## Funding

Funding for end-of-life care services is a significant issue, particularly in the light of the ageing demographic of the population and the WHO's recommendation that end-of-life care for the elderly needs to be treated as a public health issue (2004c). Without adequate funding it is impossible for clinicians to deliver the quality of holistic care implicit in palliative and end-of-life care, with its strong emphasis on symptom control, psychological, social and spiritual care, as well as family support before and after death. Funding influences not only what interventions and therapies might be available, but also what level of staffing is to be had. What is unclear from the literature is exactly what 'adequate' funding means, although the National Institute for Clinical Excellence (NICE) in its *Guidance on Cancer Services: Improving Supportive Care and Palliative Care for Adults with Cancer* (2004) established an Economic Review Group to assess the costs of providing comprehensive supportive and palliative care to people with cancer (NICE, 2004). The growing numbers of older people are projected to create increasing strain on healthcare systems, but the WHO (2004c) reports that it is often the elderly themselves who find the 'comfort care' they seek to be at odds with the more intensive, interventionist care they often receive. The WHO suggests that, rather than imagining it is necessary to seek out cheap healthcare solutions for all elderly people, the role of health may be to provide packages of care that properly take account of their wishes.

End-of-life care in the UK is divided between the independent charitable sector, social services and health services, with the independent charitable sector playing the most significant funding role until recently. Organisations such as Marie Curie Cancer Care, MacMillan Cancer Relief and other non-government organisations have provided both the infrastructure and the operational funding for hospice care. The sector is by no means uniform, with local hospices and diverse religious institutions also playing a role alongside the more wealthy and well-established charities (see discussion in *Chapter 1*). Mathew *et al* (2003) note that, despite the development of the charitable sector as expert adviser and role model, it is not 'synonymous with specialist palliative care because of the crossover in funding'. While the major charities fund some of the services that are wholly based within the NHS, the NHS also funds a small part of hospice provision. The 'market reforms' and 'purchaser–provider splits' of the Conservative 1980s meant that palliative care services and the NHS entered into contractual arrangements for end-of-life care provision (Seymour *et al*, 2002). Today, within the 'modernisation' agenda of New Labour, there is a strong emphasis on public–private partnerships, which has enmeshed these sectors even more. Social services are directly involved in end-of-life care provision because, while not able to provide specialist or complex care, they are the sector charged with providing social and home care for vulnerable older people since the introduction of the NHS and Community Care Act 1990 (Mathew *et al*, 2003).

In an attempt to quantify funds required for cancer services, each section of the NICE guidance contains an estimate or comment on the resource implications of the recommendations. For example, the set-up cost of implementing an agreed framework or managed plan of care to achieve best practice for dying patients with cancer is estimated to be £2.8million in the first year with £2.2million per annum running costs. In addition, the cost of providing full out-of-hours district nursing services in all networks is estimated to be £89.9million (NICE, 2004). Overall, in the *NHS Cancer Plan* (Department of Health, 2000), new investment monies of about £50million are promised, with the intention of matching for the first time the contribution of the voluntary sector (Seymour *et al*, 2002). This will provide a welcome injection of funds for end-of-life care, and good evaluation and quality audit, which will be discussed in *Chapter 6*, will supply data about the best way to maximise health and social expenditure on end-of-life care. However, only 17% of the 99 Health Improvement Plans surveyed by Seymour *et al* (2002) made explicit reference to the provision of palliative care for those with non-malignant disease. This suggests that, although the *NHS Cancer Plan* states that palliative care should be available for non-cancer care, it is not perceived to be a policy priority, since the targets and recommendations within the plan specifically refer to cancer patients.

In the US there are significant problems with funding end-of-life care, due in part to some of the eligibility criteria. For example, Medicare hospice care benefits have been available for people with a life expectancy of less than six months since 1982 (Price, 2003). However, only about 20% of the nation's dying ever access hospice care, and then only for a median stay of about two weeks. In a review of the literature exploring reasons for the low uptake of hospice care, Roff (2001) identifies referral procedures that are unfriendly to minority groups; limited access to comprehensive hospice care; stringent referral criteria of six months' prognosis; fiscal penalties for longer stays; and late referrals. The need for a six-month prognosis excludes many who are dying from chronic dementia, those in persistent vegitative state (PVS), and many other chronic diseases such as cardiac and respiratory disease. Such criteria confirm the longstanding bias towards cancer as the major diagnosis in palliative care, accounting for over 70% of those patients cared for by a palliative care team (Jubb, 2002). In addition, if patients accept hospice care, as part of the package under the US Medicare system, they have to agree to forgo life-sustaining medical treatments, including dialysis, radiation and chemotherapy, which may be used to provide comfort, rather than curative treatment (Roff, 2001). Furthermore, while the majority of private insurers and over 80% of managed care plans offer a hospice benefit, they do not cover palliative care in other settings, and there are significant financial disincentives to providing palliative care in acute care settings (Kyba, 2002; Reb, 2003).

The reimbursement system and level of supervision of hospice care is also a disincentive to hospice care provision. For example, under Medicare it is more financially rewarding to have nurses providing procedural interventions rather than supportive and palliative care and symptom management. This is particularly problematic for patients with dementia, where the terminal phase of the disease may take up to two years, but where home care in this phase is seen as the best option if appropriate patient and carer support is in place. Caps on home healthcare reimbursement are the norm because Medicare benefits are structured for short-term home care needs only. Because Medicare funds acute care, many dementia patients are transferred to acute care facilities and given inappropriate, aggressive care (Blasi *et al*, 2002).

In terms of supervision, in 1995 the US Office of Inspector General (OIG) investigated potential areas of fraud and abuse in relation to hospice care, specifically in relation to the six-month prognosis rule. The OIG specifically targeted hospice providers with longer lengths of stay, non-cancer diagnoses and larger numbers of nursing home enrolees (Reb, 2003). Furthermore, if a patient is in long-term care and is not being aggressively treated, the care facility may attract the state surveyor's attention for failing to restore health and rehabilitate the patient (Byock, 2001). The passage of the Medicare, Medicaid, and State Children's Health Program Benefits Improvement Act (2000) acknowledged the difficulty with the six-month prognosis rule and ordered that certification of terminal illness now be a clinician's diagnosis, rather than a timeline (Reb, 2003). However, most of the financial disincentives still exist, and access to hospice care continues to be limited.

For people who wish to die at home, much of the financial and physical stress is on the caregivers, still the 'backbone of chronic care in America' (Byock, 2001). Byock reports that the annual monetary value of informal care-giving is estimated at $196billion, compared with $32billion for home care and $83billion for nursing home care. One study reported the average loss in total wealth due to care-giving to be approximately $0.5million in aggregated wages (Metropolitan Life Insurance Company, 1999). In addition, 64% of the caregivers were employed, so employers were either losing worker time and input, supporting incomes or both.

Managed care is being suggested in America as a possible solution to the problems associated with current funding (Byock, 2001) but while some States have over 50% of Medicare enrolees in managed care plans, it is considered too soon to assess whether this will be either effective or efficient (Reb, 2003). Fiscal anomalies and discontinuity of care are deeply frustrating for clinicians who wish to provide good care at the point of delivery. Understanding the difficulties posed by funding requirements is the first step towards lobbying for change. It is essential that clinicians are aware of the funding systems that provide the framework for the practical problems they will encounter if funding is inadequate or patients are deemed ineligible for the care they need.

## The diagnosis of dying: Eligibility for palliative and end-of-life care

The decision to instigate end-of-life care as opposed to continuing with curative treatment is inextricably linked to the discussions in *Chapter 3* on refusal of active treatment, clinical decisions to forgo life-sustaining medical treatment and the relative burdens and benefits of different models of care. The question of eligibility for US Medicare hospice care has been addressed above, but there are other clinical indicators that can be used to identify the need for end-of-life care and the desirability of enrolling the patient in a palliative care pathway.

Whereas in the past the model of palliative care was that a person had curative care until they were dying, and then curative treatment was ceased and palliative treatment begun, today it is considered to be desirable that palliative care (in its broadest sense) and curative treatment are commenced

*Traditional concept of palliative care*

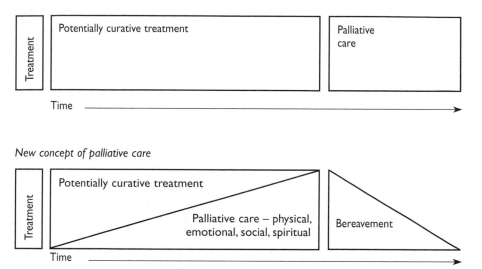

*Figure 4.1 Changing concepts of palliative care (adapted from Lynn and Adamson, 2003 in WHO, 2004a, p.15).*

simultaneously, with the former increasing as the success or need for the latter decreases, as depicted in *Figure 4.1*.

Glare and Virik (2001) have described this as the mixed management model of care. However, at some stage, palliative care turns into end-of-life care, because there is a need to focus on dying well, rather than living any longer. Once this diagnosis of dying is made, all curative care ceases, and symptom relief and psychosocial and spiritual well-being become the foci of care.

A fundamental tenet of the NHS is that appropriate care should be available to all, free at the point of service and on the basis of clinical need (Mathew *et al*, 2003). Thus the question in the UK is not whether a person can afford a particular package of care or whether their insurance covers the care, but whether they need it. That being so, there is a need to identify when end-of-life care, as opposed to palliative care, needs to be commenced, and in the past decade attention has turned to making a diagnosis of dying (Watkins, 2003). The prognosis of a terminal illness was identified in the House of Lords Select Committee First Report as being 'far from an exact science'. The Royal College of General Practitioners gave evidence that 'it is possible to make reasonably accurate prognoses of death within minutes, hours or a few days. When this stretches to months, then the scope for error can extend into years'(2005, para 117).

Notwithstanding these difficulties, care pathways for end-of-life care have been developed in the UK, with perhaps the best known developed by Ellershaw and his team at the Royal Liverpool University Hospital and the Marie Curie

Centre, known as the Liverpool Integrated Care Pathway for the Dying Patient (LCP) (Ellershaw and Murphy, 2003; NICE, 2004). The goals of the LCP will be discussed later in this chapter. The LCP uses various criteria to identify when a patient is dying from cancer. They include a reduction in consciousness, an inability to take medication, and becoming bed-bound. Ellershaw and Murphy point out that the criteria cannot always be extended to non-cancer patients, since the terminal phase might be different. For example, probable characteristics of cardiac patients who are dying include previous admissions with worsening heart failure, no identifiable reversible precipitant, receiving optimum tolerated conventional drugs, deteriorating renal function and failure to respond within two or three days to appropriate changes in diuretic or vasodilator drugs (Ellershaw and Ward, 2003). In Wales, a benchmarking study was undertaken to ascertain the effectiveness of using an integrated care pathway, modelled on the LCP, for the last two days of life. While the difficulty with predicting how long a person might be going to continue to live is evident, the criteria used to determine that a person was dying were that any two of four criteria apply. They were that the patient is: bed-bound, semi-comatose, only able to take sips of fluid, and/or no longer able to take tablets (Fowell *et al*, 2002).

An over-riding tendency to pursue active treatment and to maintain a positive attitude to clinical outcomes has been observed in both cardiologists and gerontologists, with health professionals discussing the issues among themselves but not with patients and families (Addington-Hall, 1998). In relation to the elderly, Alzheimer's disease, which contributes to an estimated 7.1% of all deaths in the USA (Allen *et al*, 2003), and is recognised as a terminal disease (Blasi *et al*, 2002), also creates difficulties in terms of a diagnosis of dying. End-stage dementia may last for up to two years, with the terminal phase marked by severe declines in functional status (bed-bound, dysphagic), severe limitations in cognitive and communicative abilities (individuals are typically mute) and susceptibility to life-threatening conditions, such as pneumonia and skin infections due to breakdown in skin integrity. In late end-stage dementia, aphasia, agnosia, apraxia and immediate and remote memory impairment are present (Allen *et al*, 2003). These signs are similar to, yet more severe than, the signs of death described in the WHO education module on palliative care for first level healthcare workers, which include decreased social interaction, decreased fluid and food intake with no hunger or thirst, changes in elimination (either reduced elimination or incontinence), respiratory changes, and circulatory changes (WHO, 2003b).

One of the clearest messages coming out of all the work on diagnosis of dying is that there must be agreement as to the diagnosis, otherwise mixed messages will be given to the patient and family and the potential for conflict and disharmony at this critical life-juncture is increased (Addington-Hall, 1998; Ellershaw and Ward, 2003; Ellershaw and Murphy, 2003; Ellershaw, 2001) Although it is clear that the diagnosis of dying presents challenges for clinicians, the positive aspect of care of the dying in the UK is that the eligibility for access to an end-of-life care pathway is still a clinical, rather than a fiscal, concern.

However, access to good palliative care seems to continue to present problems, with the House of Lords Select Committee reporting that 100 palliative care consultant posts in the UK were unfilled and that the availability of palliative care services suggested something of a 'postcode lottery' (2005, para 85).

## Location for end-of-life care

There is a range of settings where end-of-life care can be provided, from intensive care and acute hospital care at one end of the spectrum, through to nursing homes, hospice care and in the home. In most countries, the majority of older people live at home, although this varies between countries, with one in 15 people living in nursing homes in Australia and Germany, compared to one in 20 in the UK. The longer people live, the more likely they are to spend time in a nursing home, with around 50% of people aged over 80 spending some time in a nursing home in the USA (WHO, 2004c). This is, of course, only true for developed countries. In terms of preference for place of death, most studies have found that around 75% of respondents would prefer to die at home, but this number decreases if a person has recently had a personal bereavement. A systematic review of studies on preference for place of death demonstrated that when people were actually receiving care for cancer, between 50% and 70% still wished to die at home, with the numbers decreasing as death approached (Higginson and Sen-Gupta, 2000). *Cancer Pain Relief and Palliative Care*, one of the first comprehensive policy documents published on palliative care, identified five elements of fully developed palliative care programmes (WHO, 1990). They are set out in *Box 4.1.*

The reality is that many die in very different circumstances to those described above. The SUPPORT study (1995) demonstrated that Americans die in hospitals and many die hooked up to machines and in intensive care. There is significant dislocation between what people imagine they want in terms of location of end-of-life care and what they actually receive.

However, the types of illnesses people have and the facilities to support them impact on the perception and reality of the potential to die at home. The Office for National Statistics reported in 2000 that 66% of all deaths in the UK were occurring in hospitals, with only a limited number of these being in intensive care. While advanced planning may address the wishes of an increased proportion of people, there will still be people who die in intensive care units, hospital wards, nursing homes and hospices, because they, their loved ones and the clinical team feel that is the best option for care. Preference for place of

---

### Box 4.1. Elements of fully developed palliative care programmes*

■ *Home care.* Traditional medical care and funding are based on an institutional model whereas palliative care stresses the home as the primary setting for care. Institutions are seen as back-up resources rather than as the focal points of the programmes.

■ *Consultation service.* Healthcare workers who are trained in palliative care provide a consultation service for patients in hospital and in the community. Such a system also provides an educational opportunity for other healthcare workers.

■ *Day care.* Patients who live alone or who are unable to get out on their own may benefit from attending a palliative care day centre two or three times a week. In addition, day care may do much to alleviate the demands that home care makes on patients' families.

■ *Inpatient care.* Inpatient care concentrates on controlling pain and other manifestations of physical and psychosocial distress.

■ *Bereavement support.* Some people need extra help to enable them to cope with their bereavement. Support by trained healthcare workers or volunteers may provide this.

*From WHO, 1990, pp.16–17

---

death is dynamic and may change hourly, daily and with disease progression (Hinton, 1994). For example, factors such as distance and isolation may play a significant part in determining preferred place of death.

A review of studies conducted in the Northern Territory and Queensland found that while the majority of health professionals felt they would prefer to die at home and imagined their patients would prefer to do so too, the community members and patients were divided in their choices, with older people in particular preferring to die in hospital. Given the fact that many people no longer live in extended families, and that more women work full-time, family support may not be available. Indicators of preference for death in hospital include being single, older and either not having an informal carer or a lack of support for the carer (Cartwright, 2000). In other situations, a patient may already be in intensive care or an acute general ward when a decision to forgo life-sustaining medical treatment is agreed, and the relationship with the clinical staff may be such that continuity of care is better maintained by the death occurring in that unit (Campbell, 2002). Where staff have been on long-term dialysis and come to a diagnosis of end-stage renal disease, their end-of-life care is best managed between the palliative care and renal teams, with the palliative care team providing primary care, but the renal team continuing to provide support and continuity due to their longstanding relationship with the patient (Price, 2003). However, in a study on communication practices in cancer care in three countries – England, Ireland and Italy, home death was associated with less communication problems between patients and families, whereas those who died in a hospice had the largest communication problems (Higginson and Constantini, 2002), perhaps suggesting that involving families directly in end-of-life care maintains communication.

The NICE Guidance (2004) states that supportive and palliative care services should be delivered as much as possible where the patients want them, and recognises this may be in a range of settings – including home, care homes, community hospitals, hospitals and hospices. The palliative care networks, described in the National Council for Hospice and Specialist Palliative Care Services (NCHSPCS) Strategic Agenda for 2001 to 2004 (2001), are intended to provide links between people's homes, nursing and residential homes, hospices, and primary, secondary and tertiary care (Travis and Hunt, 2001). Funding from the *NHS Cancer Plan* (Department of Health, 2000) to improve communication and educational opportunities within these networks is breaking down cultural and competitive barriers in some networks in order to provide quality care in the most appropriate setting (Simpson, 2003; Pooler *et al*, 2003).

Because care at the end of life is a difficult topic for the community to contemplate, little thought is given to the issue until people are confronted with the problem. Yet the level of community dissatisfaction described in *Chapter 1* means that the public expectation of dying differs from the reality. The solution is complex and needs to be addressed through a range of strategies involving healthcare professionals, governments, educators and providers of end-of-life care. Most importantly, the community needs to determine exactly what is desirable and possible in end-of-life care, so that expectations at this critical time of life can be fulfilled.

*... Consumers have to know what good end-of-life care looks like. They have to demand it for themselves and their loved ones, and they have to know what to do when they do not get it. (Christopher, 2003)*

## Staffing and education

Given the wide variety of settings in which end-of-life care could be delivered, it is clear that not all staff delivering care will be specialist palliative care staff. The WHO document identified the fact that, although there would be specialist palliative care staff, much of the care would be provided by informal carers and non-specialist staff, with the specialist staff providing a consultancy service as required. The NICE Guidance, although addressing only the needs of cancer

---

**Box 4.2. Descriptions of different groups who might provide palliative care**

■ *Category One: Health and social care professionals providing day-to-day care to patients and families*
Refers to professionals who provide usual care to the person with cancer and their family as an integral part of their routine practice, whatever the location. For some groups of professionals, such as general practitioners and district nurses, people with cancer will not be the sole focus of their work.
■ *Category Two: Specialist palliative care*
Services in all sectors that specialise in palliative care and which includes consultants in palliative medicine, clinical nurse specialists in palliative care and a range of other specialist expertise.

From NICE, 2004, p.200

---

patients, provides the following differentiation between non-specialist and specialist staff that is equally applicable to non-cancer end-of-life settings. The descriptions are set out in *Box 4.2*.

The majority of staff caring for patients at the end of life are likely to fall into category one (see *Box 4.2*), which means that their expertise could be in renal, intensive, surgical or dementia care. In developing countries, the majority of those caring for the dying will undoubtedly be unregulated health workers, as the cost of care by health professionals would be too great (WHO, 1990). While this may not be the case in hospitals and acute care centres, in nursing homes in America (and doubtless other countries) 1.3 million unregulated nursing aides provide 80–90% of hands-on care in nursing homes. These numbers are likely to increase significantly as shortages of healthcare professionals, particularly nurses, increase (Byock, 2001). Inadequate staffing and time pressures accounted for 54% and 43% respectively of nurses' responses to the question, 'What prevents nurses from providing dignified deaths?' (Hemmings, 2003).

But palliative care is in reality only a concept, and while the specialist components of palliative care identified in *Cancer Pain Relief and Palliative Care* (WHO, 1990) may be desirable, they are by no means essential for good palliative care. What is essential is continuing professional supervision.

*Palliative care requires the involvement of a variety of healthcare workers trained to evaluate patients' needs and resources, advise patients and families, understand the principles underlying the use of drugs in pain and symptom control, and provide psychological support for both patients and families. (WHO, 1990)*

Expecting the wider emerging needs for palliative care to be met through increasing the workforce of specialist staff has been acknowledged to be unrealistic. Instead, a better solution is considered to be expanding the knowledge and skills of health professionals generally (WHO, 2004a). If these staff are to provide appropriate end-of-life care, it is clear that further education and preparation will be required to ensure that the needs of dying patients and their loved ones are appropriately addressed (NICE, 2004). Traditional pre-qualification education provided sparse information on end-of-life care, particularly in relation to communication, and it is essential that end-of-life communication education is improved (Edmonds, 1998; Kyba, 2002). Specialist education, such as intensive care unit (ICU) education, focuses almost entirely on interventionist care, but has made little room for end-of-life care in curricula in the past. Yet most nurses in ICU have regular and frequent contact with people who are dying and with their families (Campbell, 2002) and with the families of people who are pronounced brain dead (Pearson *et al*, 2001).

Similarly, district nurses (Simpson, 2003) and general practitioners (Barclay, 1998; Brown, 2002; MacLeod, 2002) are in need of specialist education to help them with issues such as symptom management (Barclay, 1998; Pooler *et al*, 2003); communication with the dying, particularly in relation to end-of-life planning (Brown, 2002; MacLeod, 2002); and spiritual care (Pooler *et al*, 2003). Pain management is of particular concern, with numerous documents outlining not only the need for clinicians to understand the need for adequate pain management generally (WHO, 1990, 1996, 2000, 2002, 2003a, b, 2004a, b, c; Pain Society, 2004a, b), but also education in end-of-life pain management techniques specifically (eg. Ellershaw and Ward, 2003, Pooler *et al*, 2003).

In order for palliative care to be implemented, a shift in philosophy needs to occur to facilitate a view of end-of-life care as a positive act, rather than as a failure (Burt, 2000). There has to be a shift in perception from a need for intensive care to a need for 'intensive caring' (Kyba, 2002). Even education about policies already in place in relation to end-of-life care activities, such as DNAR orders, may heighten awareness of the need for appropriate communication strategies (Csikai and Bass, 2000; Costello, 2002). Yet despite early deficits in end-of-life education, health professionals can further develop and even hone communication skills by continuing to attend education programmes throughout their careers (WHO, 2004a). Similarly, further education is required about pain assessment and management of symptoms, particularly in the elderly (WHO, 2004c). Zuckerman and Wollner (1999) have suggested a range of 'blended competencies' to enable clinicians educated, for example, in oncology to also study gerontology, and clinicians educated in gerontology to also study palliative care.

Numerous education initiatives have been undertaken in the past 10 years to improve the education of healthcare workers in end-of-life care. In the USA,

---

**Box 4.3 Content of education module for first-level health facility workers**

■ Assessment and treatment of the patient, including educating the family to give palliative care at home and using the caregiver booklet.
■ Management of pain, including assessment, treatment, opioid and non-opioid use, family education and special pain problems.
■ Preventative interventions, including oral care, prevention of bedsores, bathing, prevention of stiffness and contractures, and moving the bedridden patient.
■ Key symptom management, including weight loss, nausea and vomiting, mouth ulcers, pain on swallowing, dry mouth, constipation, incontinence, vaginal discharge, diarrhoea, anxiety and agitation, trouble sleeping, dementia or delirium, depression, itching, bedsores, cough, fever and hiccups.
■ Special considerations, including HIV/AIDS, ARV (antiretroviral) therapy side-effects, sexuality, children, caregivers and burnout.
■ End-of-life care, including psychosocial and spiritual support, special advice, signs of imminent death, signs of death, bereavement counselling.
■ Essential drugs.

From WHO, 2003b

---

the National Institute for Nursing Research (NINR) has provided workshops, briefings, conferences and publications on topics ranging from symptom assessment and management, pain management and gender differences to chronic illness, cultural and spiritual awareness and ethical concerns (Reb, 2003). The US private sector has also played a leading role in promoting education in end-of-life care. The Robert Wood Johnson Foundation (RWJF) funded the End-of-Life Nursing Education Consortium (ELNEC), which provides a national training programme to prepare nurse faculty members to provide end-of-life care education to students and practising nurses (Rushton and Sabatier, 2001). RWJF also funded Education for Physicians on End-of-Life Care (EPEC), which provided a range of education modules on care of the dying, including issues such as forgoing LSMT (Ackermann, 2000). There are a number of other professional groups providing education on end-of-life care funded by different benevolent organisations, including the Soros Foundation Project on Death in America (Reb, 2003). Pain management and end-of-life care questions are to be included in the national nursing licensure examination (NCLEX), and the Accreditation Council on Graduate Medical Education has included palliative care in a revised internal medicine residency programme (Reb, 2003).

In England and Wales, funding has been made available through the *NHS Cancer Plan* (Department of Health, 2000) for education of non-specialist health professionals to enable them to provide end-of-life care and is considered to be the key strategy to meet unmet need (Seymour *et al*, 2002). Funding has been obtained through these sources for district nurse education to provide home-based palliative care (Pooler *et al*, 2003; Simpson, 2003). A number of the education programmes for non-specialist care have focused on introducing the staff to integrated care pathways such as the LCP described by Ellershaw and Murphy (2003), which has been recommended in the NICE Guidance (2004) as one possible mechanism for introducing best practice care in non-specialist settings (Fowell *et al*, 2002; Pooler *et al*, 2003).

Globally, the WHO has developed an education package *Palliative Care: Symptom Management and End-Of-Life Care*, which provides advice and guidance for first-level facility health workers on the integrated management of adolescent and adult illness. The module has been developed to function as a treatment plan, and includes advice on the topics set out in *Box 4.3*.

The document is extraordinarily comprehensive and, while the sophistication of care provided by a specialist team would clearly pick up the more complex and difficult issues a dying patient may face, if all the advice in the manual were followed, there is no doubt that most patients would receive a reasonable standard of palliative care.

## Care pathways and models of care

The education module described above provides a good example of a care protocol or pathway, although it is not titled as such in the document. The NICE Guidance (2004) recommends the use of some form of clinical pathway to ensure a level of consistency in end-of-life care, and suggests that Ellershaw's LCP is one possible model. His model has been used and adapted by a number of other health providers in the UK (eg. Fowell *et al*, 2002; Batehup, 2003; Pooler *et al*, 2003; Smith *et al*, 2003) and has gained Beacon status in the UK. Beacon status is a strategy for highlighting examples of good practice in order to assist with transferability of ideas between health providers (Powell, 1999). The concept of care pathways or protocols is not without its critics, with concerns being expressed that the 'cookbook' tool discourages spontaneity and creativity, that individualised patient care will be lost, that variance analysis will be seriously flawed due to the diversity of the care providers, and that the tool may be used in future years as a measure of 'efficiency' and a means of reducing palliative care to the minimum requirements of the pathway (Burt, 2000; Kelly, 2003). Furthermore, it is argued that, since clinicians do not behave rationally in the face of dying, the use of a rational planning model is irrelevant (Burt, 2000).

---

## Box 4.4. Goals of care for patient in dying phase

*Comfort measures*

Goal 1:   Current medication assessed and non-essentials discontinued.

Goal 2:   As required, subcutaneous medication written up as per protocol.
          (Pain, agitation, respiratory tract secretions, nausea and vomiting)

Goal 3:   Discontinue inappropriate intervention.
          (Blood tests, antibiotics, intravenous fluids/medications, not for CPR
          documented, turning regimes/vital signs)

*Psychological insight*

Goal 4:   Ability to communicate in English assessed as adequate (translator not
          needed).

Goal 5:   Insight into condition assessed.

*Religious/spiritual support*

Goal 6:   Religious/spiritual needs assessed with patient/family.

*Communication with family/other*

Goal 7:   Identify how family/other are to be informed of patient's impending
          death.

Goal 8:   Family/other given relevant hospital information.

*Communication with primary healthcare team*

Goal 9:   General practitioner is aware of patient's condition.

*Summary*

Goal 10: Plan of care explained and discussed with family.

Goal 11: Family/other expresses understanding of plan of care.

From Ellershaw and Murphy, 2003, p.12

---

While there is undoubtedly a range of clinical pathways available, the purpose of this chapter is to examine the policy aspects of clinical care. Thus Ellershaw's LCP will be provided as one example of a clinical pathway, in order to understand the nature of the process, but not to suggest it to the exclusion of others. The pathway identifies the goals of care shown in *Box 4.4*.

According to Pooler *et al* (2003), who have implemented the LCP, albeit with minor adaptations, the documentation has six sections: the pathway criteria; the patient assessment form; the ongoing symptom control assessment; flow charts for symptom control; prescription and drug recording charts; and evaluation charts. Fowell *et al* (2002) also reported use of a variance sheet to identify how the care of the individual varied from the recommended pathway. Ellershaw and Murphy (2003) also present the need for DNAR documentation, which may or may not be included within the documentation described by Pooler *et al*. Presumably, once the LCP becomes an established form of documentation, the need to have separate DNAR documentation will be redundant, as DNAR will be implicit in the implementation of the pathway. From a policy perspective, it would need to be made absolutely clear in an overarching policy that, once the LCP was implemented, the expectation for other treatment and/or documentation was overridden, as medico-legal anxieties have been identified as a reason for not implementing end-of-life care (Edmonds, 1998; MacLeod, 2003). Ellershaw and Ward (2003) also recommend a range of educational resources for patients and relatives and point out that one of the advantages of the LCP is that it provides measurable outcomes of care for dying patients, which provides a foundation for evaluation of quality care.

At this point in the UK, the stated goal on the Marie Curie website in relation to the LCP is 'to build on the existing Beacon Dissemination Programme and coordinate a national model of spread and sustainability across the 34 NHS (cancer) networks' (Marie Curie website, accessed 6 October 2004). Key outcomes from implementation of the LCP to date are improved communication between primary healthcare teams and out-of-hours providers, an increase in home death rates from 11% to over 50%, improved information provided to carers, and increased professional confidence (NHS Modernisation Agency website, accessed 5 October 2004).

Organisations differ as to how to implement strategies for standardisation of end-of-life care. A range of other strategies, such as electronic charts (Childress, 2001), performance indicators for establishment and evaluation of care (Johnston and Burge, 2002), multidisciplinary team approaches (Wright, 2001), use of 'care-pair teams' of a social worker and a nurse to monitor clinical pathways (Counsell *et al*, 2003) and principle-based practice models (Ferris *et al*, 2002) all share similar characteristics to the LCP, in that they identify a set of agreed outcomes and a series of strategies to meet them, irrespective of the documentary requirements.

## Communication models and requirements

The SUPPORT study (1995) and other literature (eg. Bernabei *et al*, 1998; IOM Committee on Care at the End of Life, 1997; WHO, 2003a; Zuckerman and Wollner, 1999) not only identified problems with the quality of the physical aspects of end-of-life care, but also highlighted the need for significant improvements in doctor–patient communication. While much of the literature highlights problems with medical communication, Costello's (2002) study in the North of England demonstrates that it is also possible for nurses to support and collude with this lack of communication, albeit in this study with the 'best of intentions'. Doctor–patient communication and the need for honesty was brought into sharp relief as a result of the Kennedy Report, published in July 2001, which made public the recommendations of the public inquiry into the children's heart surgery deaths at the Bristol Royal Infirmary (Kennedy, 2001). Similarly, Higginson and Constantini identified that, in a three country study on communication in end-of-life care, communication problems were experienced by at least 10–20% of patients in relation to communication between professionals and communication of professionals to patient and family (2002, p.3680). They identified that communication was associated with quality of life issues such as 'spiritual problems, planning needs, patient insight and family insight, and, in some instances, the need to advise professionals and patient, and family anxiety' (2002, p. 3581).

Jones (2001) makes an impassioned plea for honesty in caring for patients with dementia and their expectations at end of life so that they are able to plan ahead. Clearly, in order for patients to develop advance directives or discuss refusal of treatment with their healthcare team, it is essential for them to be fully informed. Legislation such as the Patient Self-Determination Act (1990) US and the Human Rights Act (1998) UK emphasise the need for patients to be able to make informed decisions, which requires open and detailed communication from medical and nursing staff alike.

It is clear from the publication of documents such as the Hastings Center Guidelines and the Appleton Consensus (discussed in *Chapter 1*) that there was obviously strong early interest from some leaders within the medical profession to improve doctor–patient communication. Since the mid-1990s the interest in doctor–patient communication has increased, perhaps as a result of the steady stream of court cases examining the issue. There has been a plethora of position statements and advisory documents from international professional and regulatory bodies (eg. American Academy of Pediatrics, 1994; Australian Medical Association, 1997; British Medical Association, 1998; General Medical Council, 2002; British Medical Association, Resuscitation Council and Royal College of Nursing, 2003). Many of these documents spell out in considerable detail the process of a discussion about end-of-life decision making, even to the extent of suggesting not only the content of the discussion, but also pointing out within the document the need for sensitivity when discussing difficult issues, such as the possibility of forgoing a potentially life-prolonging treatment (General Medical Council, 2002). The General Medical Council goes so far as to point out that 'patients who are dying should be afforded the same respect and standard of care as all other patients'. Similar statements are the norm in these documents, not the exception, and reflect the discussion in *Chapters 2 and 3* on the need for such a focus on end-of-life care when medical technology makes it difficult for some clinicians to imagine there is not a cure for everything (Burt, 2000).

The NICE Guidance manual (2004) defines service models to ensure that people with cancer, with their families and carers, receive support and care to help them cope with cancer and its treatment at all stages. It focuses on 12 topic areas, including generalist and specialist palliative care services, physical, spiritual and social support, and continuity of care. Three chapters specifically address forms of communication. Chapter 2 focuses on user involvement in planning, delivering and evaluating services, Chapter 3 on face-to-face communication, and Chapter 4 on information. Given that the systematic review for the NICE Guidance identified that research into psychological support, specialist palliative care, information giving, and face-to-face communication has been an area of success in terms of providing an evidence base for practice (National Cancer Research Institute, 2004) there would appear still to be a need to translate the research into practice.

Three levels of communication are required (Counsell *et al*, 2003). Firstly, communication between the disciplines and leaders of the healthcare organisation to ensure that the policies underpinning the end-of-life care programme are in place. Secondly, communication between members of the healthcare team to ensure all members of the multidisciplinary team agree on the decision, as well as the doctor and the patient (Ellershaw, 2001; Ellershaw and Ward, 2003). Collaboration is the key to successful healthcare outcomes (Zuckerman and Wollner, 1999; Glare and Virik, 2001; Pooler *et al*, 2003), and all members of the team need to have their opinions recognised in proportion to their level of experience and knowledge of the patient. While individual clinicians are reported to (Costello, 2002; Pooler *et al*, 2003) and some organisations expressly state (BMA, Resuscitation Council and the Royal College of Nursing, 2003; Pain Society, 2004b) support for the notion of physician primacy in end-of-life (and other) aspects of care, there is an increasing recognition that a range of health professionals may have the most accurate knowledge of the patient and may in fact be managing and co-ordinating the patient's care (Byock, 2003). In some cases this may be a district nurse (Pooler *et al*, 2003), in others a long-term specialist nurse practitioner (Price, 2003), in others a general practitioner (Brown, 2002) and in others a social worker (Csikai and Bass, 2000; Counsell *et al*, 2003), Thirdly, there is the need to communicate carefully with the patient and family members and loved ones, in order to ensure that there are no misunderstandings about exactly what is to happen.

The need to document discussions and care is an ongoing requirement in modern health practice, and is repeatedly highlighted in advisory documents and other literature, specifically in relation to sensitive discussions such as forgoing LSMT (Hastings Center, 1987; Appleton Consensus, 1992; General Medical Council, 2002) or DNAR (BMA, Resuscitation Council and Royal College of

Nursing, 2003). The need for 'clear and convincing evidence' of patients' wishes in relation to end-of-life care was brought into focus by the Cruzan case (1990) (see *Chapter 2*) and has now been included in much of the advance directive legislation in the US (Scanlon, 2003) and Australia (Mendelson, 1999).

England and Wales have not legislated for this requirement, although the common law has recognised that advance directives, when written, are binding on clinicians and have legal status (Dimond, 2001). A difficulty for clinicians is that, if no rationalisation of documentation occurs, the documents required for end-of-life care, such as advance directives, DNAR orders and integrated clinical pathways become another set of documentation overlaying the paperwork they already have to do. This is a serious consideration for policymakers in end-of-life care. Documentation is clearly critical in order to record these sensitive and emotional decisions for two reasons: firstly, to ensure that good care is communicated to all caregivers in order to ensure both continuity of care and consistent quality of care; and secondly, to ensure accurate documentation in case of challenge by distressed or dissatisfied relatives or other interested parties (Chiarella, 1995a). However, if clinicians do not perceive these records to be their priority in terms of documentation, it is unlikely that they will complete them accurately. It is thus incumbent upon policymakers and organisational leaders to determine how documentation is rationalised as more healthcare records are introduced.

## Conclusion

This chapter has set out a range of policy issues that directly impact on clinical practice. The chapter began by examining funding for end-of-life care, which clearly requires significant revision in the USA, but is not so problematic in the UK due in most part to the philosophy of the NHS in relation to free access to healthcare at the point of delivery. The diagnosis of dying appreciably influences the eligibility of patients to access end-of-life care and these complex clinical issues are currently receiving scrutiny. Both funding and diagnosis of dying impact significantly on the location for end-of-life care, which in turn affects the staff available to deliver the care and the education they will require. The policy consequences of new models of care delivery and clinical pathways have been touched upon, as has the need for improved communication and documentation. It is clear that a comprehensive revision of policy and documentation will be necessary if end-of-life care is to be seen as a central plank of healthcare delivery, rather than as an addition at the end of life.

# CHAPTER 5

# Snapshot of international developments

This chapter provides a snapshot of palliative care in a number of developing or developed countries in order to provide an understanding of the comparative progress and growth of end-of-life care. An edition of the *Journal of Pain and Symptom Management* in 2002 contained a collection of reports from a diverse range of countries on the development of palliative care and cancer services. This has provided a valuable and significant, although not exclusive, resource for this chapter. This chapter does not attempt to provide a comprehensive review of palliative care in Europe as this work has been undertaken by Henk ten Have and David Clark (2002). Rather, it provides analyses of palliative and end-of-life care in other countries to expand the understanding of policy influences.

## The influence of the WHO on global developments in end-of-life care

The need to develop national frameworks for palliative and end-of-life care was highlighted by the WHO in its 1990 publication *Cancer Pain Relief and Palliative Care* and, although until recently most of the focus has been predominantly on cancer care, there is no doubt that the WHO has been the main co-ordinator of palliative and end-of-life care globally, and a major stimulus for the development of many national palliative and end-of-life care delivery services. This was discussed from a historical perspective in *Chapter 1*. In reviewing the development of palliative and end-of-life care services in different countries, it is clear that there is huge variation, particularly between developing and developed countries. However, there is still significant disparity between countries of similar wealth and it is clear that political will and subsequent government policy are major factors in the establishment of strong and accessible palliative and end-of-life care services (Sepulveda *et al*, 2002).

*Table 5.1* provides an overview of the various countries discussed in the literature. The table highlights in particular the availability of palliative and end-of-life care as core government programmes, the presence or absence of a policy or legislative framework, the presenting conditions of the patient population seeking palliative and end-of-life care services, who else might

**Table 5.1. Palliative and end-of-life care development by country and author**

| Country and author | Population | Provision of PC as a core service by government | PC provided by | Legislation or policy framework for PC | Presenting conditions of patient population | Barriers/ ongoing issues | WHO involvement or recognition |
|---|---|---|---|---|---|---|---|
| *Argentina* (Wenk and Bertolino, 2002; Bruera and Sweeney, 2002) | 35million | No | NGOs, 70–90 Government funded PC teams | PC now recognised as an area of medical practice by Government resolution | Mainly cancer patients, some AIDS, some chronic care (but very small numbers) | Funding due to currency devaluation Opioid accessibility Education Public information | Cited in references |
| *Canada* (Bruera and Sweeney, 2002; Ferris et al, 2002) | 27.5million | Yes, but still only accessed by a minority | Government, NGOs, religious organisations | National Delphi study to build consensus on PC model of care | 80–90% of patient population with cancer, slightly younger group access hospice care | Not too many, mainly need for increase and spread of PC programmes | Cited in references |
| *Italy* (Ventafridda, 2002) | Not stated | Yes, both hospice care and home care in theory | Government, NGOs, charitable and voluntary | Since 1988 one hospice required per region of Italy | Mainly cancer | Improved pain management and opioid use (still very low – | Cited in references |

| | | | | | | | |
|---|---|---|---|---|---|---|---|
| | | In practice, poor commitment to PC | sectors | | | lowest morphine use in Europe in 1999. Public education | |
| *Japan* (Takeda, 2002; Masuda et al, 2003) | Not stated | Yes, Government orchestrated campaign following WHO involvement | Government, some NGOs | Legislative and policy framework revised in 1992 | 1 in 3 people in Japan die of cancer | Opioid consumption still low for a developed country Cultural and judicial resistance to advance directives | WHO directly involved and worked with Government in 1990s on cancer pain management and education |
| *Lebanon* (Daher et al, 2002) | 4million | No, only 465 out of 15 000 patients treated for palliative care and pain management in public facilities | Mostly private healthcare. Government has 8 trained fellows due to WHO intervention | Not described – seems unlikely | Fellows have focused on cancer patients but need to focus on AIDS Chronic diseases and dementia recognised | Lack of morphine availability and restricted legislation Lack of reimbursement for PC work No referral system | WHO provided workshops, funding and education Significant intervention |

| Country and author | Population | Provision of PC as a core service by government | PC provided by | Legislation or policy framework for PC | Presenting conditions of patient population | Barriers/ongoing issues | WHO involvement or recognition |
|---|---|---|---|---|---|---|---|
| *Lithuania* (Seskevicius, 2002) | 3.5million | Government manages cancer treatment fully, but PC not included in 2001/2002 policy documents | Two Government funded pain clinics, NGOs, benevolent sector, eg. Open Society Institute | Yes 2002 legislation passed to improve opioid availability, also reference to WHO in 2003–2010 policy | 70% of cancer patients require pain management and PC | Many people too poor to buy medication State regulations still limit opioid availability Further education needed | Government endorses use of WHO pain management guidelines for 2003–2010 policy |
| *Mongolia* (Davaasuren, 2002) | 2.4million | No | Soros Foundation funds PC department with 10 beds Family care for dying | Not mentioned but obviously restrictions on opioid prescription | Mainly cancer patients who present very late 61% die within first year | 41% of cancer patients die at home without treatment Not a medical specialty No education GPs cannot prescribe opioids | WHO Guidelines have been translated into Mongolian |

| | | | | | | | |
|---|---|---|---|---|---|---|---|
| *New Zealand* (MacLeod, 2001) | 3.8million | Yes, PC Government funded but still developing | Local community-based hospices, Government health services volunteers Most die at home | Policy – NZ PC Strategy 2001 | 90% have cancer | Need for improved education Need for greater public understanding | Not mentioned |
| *Netherlands* (Cohen-Almagor, 2002; House of Lords Select Committee Report, 2005) | 16million | Yes, improving Government approach to PC Care of dying mainly home care provided by GPs PC still not integrated well into nursing care | Government, nursing homes, GPs (although 90% of GPs admit to practising PAS or euthanasia) | Legalisation of PAS and euthanasia (2001) led to increased Government focus on PC to address community concerns | Not described in terms of PC (long list of different patients who had been euthanised) | Record keeping Relationship between PAS and PC Lack of academic development of PC | Cited in references |
| *Norway* (Kaasa et al, 2002) | Not stated | Yes, fully Government funded since 1990s | Government funded hospice care, some NGO support | Strong policy base | Not described | Need for extra funding Need for specialist PC curriculum | Policy programme based on WHO definition |

| Country and author | Population | Provision of PC as a core service by government | PC provided by | Legislation or policy framework for PC | Presenting conditions of patient population | Barriers/ ongoing issues | WHO involvement or recognition |
|---|---|---|---|---|---|---|---|
| *Poland* (Luczak et al, 2002) | 38.6million | Yes | State funds plus voluntary hospice movement | Strong policy and legislative base | Mainly cancer | Need for improved opioid availability and prescribing policies | WHO guidelines used as basis for education |
| *Romania* (Mosoiu, 2002) | 22.4million | No, local policy is on curing cancer, no focus on PC or pain management | NGO and UK-based voluntary sector | WHO working with Government to develop policy | Mainly cancer where available | Lack of opioid availability Need for education Need for recognition of PC as specialty | WHO centrally involved in policy development |
| *Spain* (Bruera and Sweeney, 2002; Batiste et al | 40million (Catalonia 6.2million) | Yes, but not uniform in applicability | NGOs, religious organisations, private companies Catalonia: | Government policy established in Catalonia to implement and support | Mainly cancer sufferers Also AIDS and elderly on increase in Catalonia | Opioid use low overall (strong in Catalonia) Need to improve co-ordination | WHO funded demonstration project in Catalonia Both authors cited in |

| | | | Government and WHO | demonstration programme | | of services | references |
|---|---|---|---|---|---|---|---|
| (Catalonia). 2002 | | | | | | | |
| Turkey (Oguz et al, 2003) | Not stated | No | Mainly family care for the dying with some Government home services in place | A patients' bill of rights has been developed | No PC services so no real client group identified | Home care problems Lack of narcotics Lack of healthcare professional education Isolation of dying patients | WHO Declaration of Alma-Ata cited in policy |
| Uganda Stjernsward, 2002; WHO, 2004) | 23.3million | Ministry of Health has included relief of pain and PC in home care package, but care provided by NGO | Nurses, family members, home and community-based organisations NGO (TASO) | Strong policy plan, due to inclusion in WHO community health programme | AIDS mainly then cancer | Accessibility to healthcare, only 50% of people will ever see a doctor or nurse Insufficient morphine supplies for home care | Major WHO support programme |

NGO, Non-governmental organisation; PC, palliative care; TASO, The AIDS Support Organisation; WHO, World Health Organisation be providing the services if the government is not, what barriers exist to the provision of palliative and end-of-life care services, and whether or not there was a mention or recognition of the role of the WHO.

The inclusion of a column recording any reference to the WHO in the literature is in recognition of the impact on policy the intervention and/or support of the WHO is able to achieve. While it is acknowledged that the WHO is not without its critics, particularly recently in relation to its listing of HIV drugs for use in developing countries (Lee, 2004), nevertheless the articles reviewed for this chapter demonstrate the impact WHO policy has had on palliative and end-of-life care. A comparison of the success of palliative and end-of-life care services in Catalonia, where the WHO Demonstration Programme was introduced (Gomez-Batiste *et al*, 2002) with the overall implementation of palliative and end-of-life care services nationally in Spain (Bruera and Sweeney, 2002) demonstrates the effectiveness of good policy implementation and education of healthcare professionals. Following the introduction of the programme in Catalonia, the use of hospital emergency wards to care for dying patients had fallen from 52% in 1993 to 3.3% in 2002. By 2002 the direct coverage for cancer was 67.1%, the geographical coverage was 91%, the mean basal pain score was a low 2.9 using a visual analogue scale, and morphine consumption has risen dramatically. The introduction of this programme has meant

**Table 5.2. Important issues related to palliative care in developing and developed countries**

| Developing countries | Developed countries |
|---|---|
| Poverty | Insufficient knowledge of healthcare professionals |
| Insufficient knowledge of healthcare professionals | Integration between hospital-based and community care |
| Patients and families receiving inadequate information about diagnosis or prognosis | Funding for community care |
| Drug availability | Communication with patients and families |
| Lack of models for delivery of palliative care | Lack of national/regional policies for palliative care |
| From Bruera and Sweeney, 2002, p.324 | |

reduction in hospital length of stay, emergency usage and death in hospital, with costs shifting from acute care to palliative care and home care support teams in the first 10 years (Gomez-Batiste *et al*, 2002). The series of workshops conducted by the WHO around the world had significant impact on the development of palliative and end-of-life care services, and the workshops are often mentioned specifically within the articles as being the catalysts for change.

## Differences between developed and developing countries

The issues are significantly different for countries with large populations and/or limited resources. *Table 5.2* identifies resources as ongoing barriers to implementation of national policy and highlights the differences in the extent of integration of palliative care into core services between developed and developing countries. Bruera and Sweeney (2002) identify a number of differing issues of importance related to palliative care in developed and developing countries. Although the lack of knowledge of health professionals and the need for improved communication straddle both developed and developing countries, the issues of poverty and drug availability are of monumental significance for developing countries and surpass all other concerns.

## Prerequisites for national policy

The Expert Committee on Cancer Pain Relief and Active Supportive Care identified the first prerequisite for a national policy on palliative and end-of life care as the need to recognise that cancer pain and other common cancer symptoms are under-treated. The three planks of any policy designed to implement palliative and end-of-life care are:

■ A commitment to train healthcare workers to manage pain and other common symptoms.
■ A commitment to ensure availability of opioid and non-opioid analgesics.
■ A commitment to develop a legislative and policy framework (WHO, 1990).

It is clear from the barriers to implementation of palliative and end-of-life care identified in *Table 5.1* that those prerequisites are as critical today as when first identified. Bruera and Sweeney (2002) elaborate on those prerequisites. They explain that the need for education incorporates education of the public, patients and family, and healthcare professionals and leaders. Legislation needs to address access to and funding of care and monitoring of effectiveness. Drug availability includes the need for an essential formulary, changes in legislation and regulations to improve availability (especially for opioids) and monitoring of price and access.

# The impact of resource availability on palliative and end-of-life care

The availability of resources clearly impacts on the implementation of palliative and end-of-life care, as scarce resources must be matched against demand, and people who are dying may not be accorded the same level of priority as those who have the possibility of survival. But informal caring for the dying also impacts significantly on the human resources of a nation, as the duration of bed-ridden care for the terminally ill in developing countries is 3–6 months, which has significant impact on the families and informal carers of the dying (WHO, 2004b).

The WHO has recently developed a series of models for national cancer control activities based on resource realities (WHO, 2002). These scenarios or models are identified for countries with a low, medium or high level of resources and attempt to match possible activity to control cancer according to the political, epidemiological and socio-economic situations in a country at any given time.

### National policy for countries with a low level of resources

Where there is only a low level of resources, the WHO recommends that the government ought to 'establish a basis for prevention of cancer and other diseases by limiting the extent to which the scourges of the industrialised world – tobacco use and the "western" diet – can enter the country'. National diagnosis and treatment guidelines might help the general public and healthcare workers to be aware of the early warning signs of cancer and other diseases. But the most significant contribution in terms of palliative and end-of-life care would be 'to establish a basis for pain relief and palliative care of individuals with advanced disease to ensure they maintain as high as possible quality of life' (WHO, 2002). This is clearly the aim in the community health approach to palliative care for HIV/AIDS and cancer patients in sub-Saharan Africa (WHO, 2004). This project, which aims to 'improve the quality of life for HIV/AIDS patients in sub-Saharan Africa by developing palliative care programmes with a public health approach', has five countries participating – Botswana, Ethiopia, United Republic of Tanzania, Uganda and Zimbabwe – and has relatively modest goals for the first phase. These goals require the participating countries to complete team development and project proposals, obtain political support from their governments and to start networking and collaborating, especially around policy development. In those countries to date, only Botswana has an operational home-based care programme integrated into the national health system, although the Ministry of Health in Uganda has included relief of pain and palliative care in its home care package. However, even in Botswana 28% of caregivers interviewed were dissatisfied with the quality of care they were able to deliver, mainly due to inadequate treatment or symptom control. Ethiopia has no government programme and very few non-government programmes, and in the United Republic of Tanzania, non-government and voluntary agencies provide the majority of services. Zimbabwe's home-based care programme also is provided mainly by private organisations. (WHO, 2004b). Only the Ugandan Government is discussed within the literature reviewed in *Table 5.1* (Stjernsward, 2002).

Other countries, while not experiencing the problems of HIV/AIDS to the same extent as Africa, are nevertheless extremely poor and lacking in resources. For example, in Mongolia, cancer is the second largest cause of death after cardiovascular disease, and over 62% of cancer patients were diagnosed very late and were incurable. Most people diagnosed at this stage would be discharged home with no palliative care to suffer from unmanaged pain and other symptoms. There are very few analgesic drugs available and family doctors cannot prescribe opioids. There was no education for health professionals in palliative care at under- or post-graduate level (Davaasuren, 2002).

However, in its 2003 grant rounds the Open Society Institute of the Soros Foundation provided $20 000 to the National Medical University of Mongolia to support the development of a resource training centre in palliative care for Mongolia and a further $3750 to support follow-up activities of the Mongolian team who participated in the Budapest Palliative Care Policy Development Workshop in October, 2003. In 2004 the Mongolian Foundation for Open Society reported the establishment of a five-day national trainers' training of palliative care. The training is organised by the Palliative Care Association of Mongolia as a result of the Open Society grant and is designed for the teaching staff of public and private medical and nursing schools and colleges throughout of Mongolia. Thirty-five teachers studied theoretical and practical aspects of palliative care at an advanced level, to institutionalise palliative care education. This year on World Hospice and Palliative Care Day, several major events were held in Mongolia through this funding in order to raise awareness of palliative care.

## National policy for countries with a medium level of resources

Countries with a medium level of resources are described by the WHO (2002) as often having a large urban population and a life expectancy of over 60 years, with cancer being one of the leading causes of death. Furthermore, there is often a high exposure to risk factors such as tobacco, diet, infectious diseases and carcinogens in the workplace. The infrastructure for cancer services, including palliative and end-of-life care is in place, but services are often limited in quantity, quality and accessibility. Primary prevention and early detection are limited in favour of treatment. Lithuania and Romania fit within these descriptions out of the countries reviewed in *Table 5.1*. However, despite the fact that the Government in Lithuania fully funds cancer treatment services, including a cancer registry, large numbers of cancer patients do not present until Stage 4 when their disease is advanced and incurable, as 70% of cancer patients require palliative care and pain management (Seskevicius, 2002). Romania has also had a national programme on cancer control and prevention since 1980, but still, more than two-thirds of cancer patients are diagnosed in the late stages of their disease (Mosoiu, 2002).

The WHO recommends that countries such as these focus on primary prevention activities such as tobacco control, reduction of alcohol use and promotion of health, diet and physical exercise. Infectious agents and workplace hazards also require attention. In terms of screening, if cervical cancer rates are high, then screening for cervical cancer should be introduced, but screening for other types should be discontinued in favour of treating curable cancers and conducting clinical trials for cost-effectiveness of treatments. Radiotherapy and chemotherapy should be introduced only into specialised centres and pain relief and palliative care, using low cost drugs such as oral morphine, should be a priority (WHO, 2002). In Lithuania, there is no shortage of opioid analgesics, but it is difficult for poor people to purchase the medication unless it is covered by the State health insurance fund. Similarly, because prescriptions can only be issued for seven days and the rules around prescribing opioids are 'quite complicated', some cancer patients do not receive adequate analgesia due to prescribing restrictions (Seskevicius, 2002). In Romania, oral morphine was not available in 2002, and the laws governing opioid prescription had not changed from 1969. Both patients and health professionals were in need of education about opioid usage in order to reduce barriers to adequate pain relief (Mosoiu, 2002).

Other countries, which might in some aspects be considered to fit into this medium level of resource availability, do not seem to provide services even as well as Lithuania or Romania. For example, Lebanon, which has six universities with medical and nursing schools, only provides Government-funded palliative care through the auspices of nine fellows who in turn received their educational funding through an anonymous donor. These fellows were providing the great majority of opioid medication in Lebanon at the time of the report (Daher *et al*, 2002). Similarly Turkey has an emphasis on the treatment of disease, and an overcrowded secondary specialist system. There are very few public nursing homes, with most care being provided through private agencies, to which the poor have no access. Despite the emphasis on treatment, only 8.4% of the population lives to be over 60, with the majority dying in hospital without pain management. There is no organisation or training around palliative and end-of-life care (Oguz *et al*, 2003). Argentina might also (just) be considered to fall into this medium resource category, but they have virtually no public infrastructure for palliative care, with the majority of patients with advanced incurable disease being mismanaged and their symptoms going uncontrolled. Opioid availability is limited, particularly as a result of the currency devaluation, which has put the cost of opioids out of reach of the majority of the population (Wenk and Bertolino, 2002).

## National policy for countries with a high level of resources

Countries with a high level of resources are described as being countries with life expectancy over 70 years of age, with cancer being a major cause of death for both men and women. Although many elements of a cancer control programme exist, they may be neither well integrated into a national system nor evenly distributed, with particular groups such as rural and indigenous populations being under-serviced (WHO, 2002).

For these countries, comprehensive health promotion programmes are recommended, including in schools and workplaces, in order to promote awareness of early warning signs of cancer. However, the WHO still only recommends screening for breast and cervical cancer, as other forms have not yet demonstrated cost-effectiveness. In terms of curative treatment, the network of comprehensive cancer treatment centres that are active for clinical training and research needs to be reinforced, with special support given to the ones acting as national and international reference centres. The inability of these countries to provide easy access to pain relief and palliative care is highlighted as being on ongoing problem, as was indicated by the SUPPORT study (1995) and others (see *Chapter 1*), despite high levels of resources.

When examining the countries that fit into this resource rich category, Canada, Italy, Japan, New Zealand, Norway and Spain all report having palliative and end-of-life services which are core to their government programmes. Norway (Kaasa *et al*, 2002) and Poland (Luczak *et al*, 2002) seem to have been particularly proactive in establishing core services which address many of the end-of-life care needs of their citizens, and meet the

WHO (1990) requirements for palliative care services. However, they too report the need for more education for healthcare professionals and Poland is concerned to improve prescribing policies regarding opioids. In Canada (Ferris *et al*, 2002; Bruera and Sweeney, 2002), and New Zealand (MacLeod, 2001), where comprehensive and consistent palliative care services are part of a national strategy, there is still difficulty in accessing all elements of the community equally. In Canada this is partly due to governmental inconsistencies, as different provinces have in the past had different approaches to palliative care (Ferris *et al*, 2002; Bruera and Sweeney, 2002). In New Zealand, the indigenous (Maori) population had particular difficulties in accessing adequate palliative care services (MacLeod, 2001). Several countries still report less than optimal usage of opiates, although most report that this is improving. Italy in particular (Ventafridda, 2002), but also Spain (Bruera and Sweeney, 2002) report low opioid usage in comparison to other resource rich countries (WHO, 1996). Japan has made significant progress since the intervention of the WHO in the mid-1990s, but still reports lower than expected usage of opioids (Takeda, 2002) and some cultural objection to issues such as advance directives, which the doctors do not always regard and the courts do not uphold (Masuda *et al*, 2003).

## The possible impact of the legalisation of PAS and euthanasia

The Netherlands is of particular interest, as it has been proactive originally in the decriminalisation of euthanasia, and more recently in the passing of the Termination of Life on Request and Assistance with Suicide Act of 2001, which legalises physician-assisted suicide (PAS) and voluntary euthanasia (VE). Three categories of doctor can provide PAS and VE: general practitioners (GPs), nursing home doctors and specialists. Over 90% of GPs had either performed euthanasia or would be willing to do so, whereas only 3% of all specialist deaths were attributable to euthanasia. Furthermore, only one-fifth of all nursing home doctors had ever honoured a request (Cohen-Almagor, 2002). Eighty to ninety percent of all patients requesting euthanasia are cancer patients. In a survey undertaken following the passing of the Termination of Life on Request and Assistance with Suicide Act (2001), there was significant division among experts as to whether the legalisation of PAS has influenced the provision of palliative and end-of-life care for better or worse. Those who consider it has had a detrimental effect believe that the focus on euthanasia has overshadowed the focus on palliative care. They argue that, since the majority of people die at home in the care of their GP, and GPs are the group of clinicians most likely to perform PAS, the most probable outcome for them has been euthanasia or PAS.

Those who believe it has had a positive impact argue that all doctors receive education in palliative care and are encouraged to offer palliative care before euthanasia. However, perhaps because most patients die at home, there was consensus among the experts interviewed that palliative care was not adequately integrated into hospital nursing services and education (Cohen-Almagor, 2002). Thus, even in a resource-rich country that is considered by many to be advanced in core policy for palliative and end-of-life care, there is still a problem with the education for health professionals. Switzerland has also legalised assistance in dying, but here the assistance does not have to be given by a medical practitioner. Anyone can provide assistance, providing their motives are honourable and they do not stand to profit from their actions (House of Lords Select Committee, 2005). Belgium also passed legislation in 2002 that legalised voluntary euthanasia, but not assistance in dying, physician-assisted or otherwise. For an extensive account of the impact of assistance in dying and voluntary euthanasia legislation on the various jurisdictions and associated practices, refer to Chapter 5 of the House of Lords Select Committee Report. The Oregon experience in terms of legalised PAS is also described in detail in the House of Lords Select Committee Report and has been discussed in this text in *Chapter 3*. Although the impact on the provision of palliative and end-of-life care in Oregon seems to be limited to date (Miller, 2000), the implementation of the legislation is still in its very early stages and a review at 10 years will be more helpful.

## Conclusion

This chapter has provided a snapshot of the literature on palliative and end-of-life care in countries with differing levels of resources. It has undertaken to provide an overview of the literature in table form and to use the WHO (2002) recommendations on matching resources to national cancer control activities to categorise the countries according to resource availability. While there is significant variation between the extent to which countries have implemented palliative and end-of-life care programmes, there is a consistent need to educate health professionals and the public and to improve access to opioids for the terminally ill.

# CHAPTER 6

# Future directions for policy and research

## Introduction

This final chapter brings together the recommendations from the documents reviewed within this manuscript in terms of future national and local policy development and research directions. This book has analysed international and national political and policy documents, new pieces of legislation, ground-breaking case law and correspondingly strong opinion within the health, law and ethics literature. Such changes inevitably lead to policy innovations, which in turn need to be underpinned by a strong evidence base. Many of these developments are relatively recent, and thus at first instance there is a need not only for a limited range of clinical research in terms of pharmacotherapies, but also, equally importantly in this field for descriptive and evaluative research, to describe and assess the impact of these changes on both the patients and the health professionals.

The chapter begins with a review of what patients and carers want from end-of-life care, and then looks at policy development and implementation, including educational needs and consumer involvement. Research and evaluation directions are then considered. These elements of the future directions for end-of-life care are not separate, but integrated, as demonstrated in *Figure 6.1*.

*Figure 6.1* identifies the integration between policy development and implementation, and their relationship to education, research and community involvement. Each informs the other. Education, research and community involvement are clearly elements of policy development and implementation, but at the same time, education, research and community involvement will inform and shape policy development and implementation. Furthermore, in each component of the work there is the need for evaluation, which will also sculpt and update policy development and implementation.

## What patients and carers want and need

The NICE publication *Guidance on Cancer Services: Improving Supportive and Palliative Care for Adults with Cancer* (2004) (the NICE Guidance)

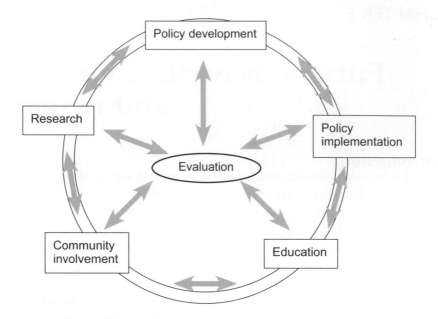

*Figure 6.1. Integration of policy and research.*

sets out to define service models to ensure that people with cancer, with their families and carers, receive support and care to help them cope with cancer and its treatment at all stages. It is based on a service model involving cancer networks as the vehicles for delivering the desired outcomes. Cancer networks are defined as

> *Partnerships of organisations (both statutory and voluntary) working to secure the effective planning, delivery and monitoring of cancer services, including those for supportive and palliative care. They provide the framework for developing high quality services by bringing together relevant health and social care professionals, service users and managers.*

The NICE Guidance begins by outlining what the research to date indicates that patients and carers want and need in relation to end-of-life care. Fourteen key issues are identified and listed in *Box 6.1.*

These wants and needs provide an excellent foundation for any consideration of future policy and research. There can be no better reasons to develop policy or to undertake research than either to supply the infrastructure to provide for these wants and needs or to search for methods to improve strategies to meet them.

> ### Box 6.1. Wants and needs of patients and carers
>
> - To be treated as individuals.
> - To have their voice heard, to be valued for their knowledge and skills and to be able to exercise real choice about treatments and services.
> - To receive detailed, high quality information about their disease and possible treatment, given in an honest, timely and sensitive manner at all stages of the patient pathway.
> - To know what options are available to them under the NHS, voluntary and independent sectors, including access to self-help and support groups, complementary therapy services and other information.
> - To know they will only undergo those interventions for which they have given informed consent.
> - To have good face-to-face communication with healthcare professionals.
> - To know that services will be well-coordinated.
> - To know that services will be of high quality.
> - To know that their physical symptoms will be managed to a degree that is acceptable to them and is consistent with their clinical situation and clinicians' current knowledge and expertise.
> - To receive emotional support from professionals who are prepared to listen to them and are capable of understanding their concerns.
> - To receive support and advice on financial and employment issues.
> - To receive support to enable them to explore spiritual issues.
> - To die in the place of their choice.
> - To be assured that their family and carers will be supported throughout the illness and in bereavement.
>
> From NICE, 2004, pp.15–16

## Policy development and implementation

The challenge for governments and organisations who seek to provide end-of-life care is to make a more concerted effort to improve care by concentrating on proven strategies based on the patient and carer needs and the complexity of the illness at any given point in time (WHO, 2004c). Responsibility for the care of people at the end of life can be viewed as a quality indicator for governments. As the WHO (2004a) has observed

*People who are dying are among the most vulnerable, and the quality of care they receive must be one mark of society's humanity as a whole.*

Byock (2001) identified the precepts of hospice and palliative care as being: ethical decision making that respects patient autonomy and the role of family or legal surrogates; an interdisciplinary team approach to care; patient and family as the unit of care; effective and (when necessary) intensive symptom management; dying understood as a time of life, with improving quality of life as a primary goal; recognition of the importance of the 'inner life' of the person; and bereavement support to the family during the initial period of grieving. These precepts correspond closely with the needs and wants identified by NICE, but also provide a clearer indication of the policy infrastructure required to meet them. In the document *Better Palliative Care for Older People*, the WHO (2004c) identified a number of barriers to be removed before good palliative and end-of-life care (in this case for older people) can become a central plank of government policy, and not just an 'add-on extra'. The barriers include:

- A lack of awareness and knowledge of the scale of the problem.
- A lack of health policies for palliative care, both for older people and for the diseases they commonly suffer from.
- A lack of integration of palliative care across healthcare settings and services.
- A lack of palliative care ethos or skills in the settings where older people are actually cared for and die.
- Complacency and age discrimination about the need to provide high-quality end-of-life care for older people.
- Faulty assumptions about the needs of older people and their desire or ability to cope without special forms of help.
- Failure to implement simple proven effective measures.
- The complexity of linking care packages across different settings and between health and social support and care.
- A lack of resources and outdated patterns of care and health systems delivery.

These barriers will need to be addressed by implementation of policy to overcome them, community and health professional education to enable changes in attitudes and improvement in knowledge, research to provide awareness of the scale of the problem and best practice, and evaluation of strategies to ensure effectiveness and efficiency (WHO, 2004c).

There is consensus from a policy perspective about the need to have end-of-life care treated as a public health issue (WHO 2004a, 2004c; NICE, 2004; EURAG, 2004). In order to achieve this change, governments will be required to identify needs within populations, monitor trends and the effectiveness of interventions, increase professional education and public awareness, and set up systems that can support the changes needed in behaviour and practice (WHO, 2004c). NICE recommends that the Department of Health and the Welsh Assembly should oversee the implementation of the Guidance by developing standards related to supportive and palliative care that reflect the Guidance.

Policy makers need to undertake a range of activities in order to implement a public health approach to end-of-life care. Many of the policy recommendations focus on funding, rewarding and supporting quality palliative care services, including symptom management, communication skills and co-ordination of care. Others stress the need to act against ageist stereotypes that may inhibit the provision of palliative care to older people. This may require anti-discrimination legislation. The co-ordination of care between the public, private and not-for-profit sectors is also seen to be critical (WHO, 2004c).

The need for continuous improvement of palliative and end-of-life care services is a recurrent feature of policy, and is identified in the WHO document *Palliative Care: The Solid Facts* (2004a). The 'plan-do-study-act' (PDSA) cycle is suggested as a possible framework for quality improvement. This improvement model is an iterative process based on three key questions: What are we trying to accomplish, how will we know that a change is an improvement; and what changes can we make that will result in an improvement? (Langley *et al*, 1996). In order to implement such a framework, the WHO recommends that policy makers should reward healthcare organisations that engage in audit and quality improvement schemes in palliative care, disseminate examples of good practice and constantly review their success in palliative care (2004a). The Liverpool Integrated Care Pathway (Ellershaw and Murphy, 2003) is cited as an example of good practice that could be used to make an improvement (NICE, 2004). NICE also charges the Department of Health and the Welsh Assembly with responsibility for ensuring quality programmes are in place to monitor progress towards achieving its recommendations and for ensuring mechanisms are in place to monitor changes over time in patients' experiences of care. In terms of continuous review and audit of quality palliative and end-of-life care, EURAG (2004), in its draft *Decision of the Council of the European Union*, recommends that member states undertake regular reviews to ascertain the extent to which palliative and end-of-life care has been integrated into mainstream care delivery services. The House of Lords Select Committee First Report identified that access to adequate palliative care is a 'postcode lottery' (2005, para 85).

What is not discussed in any of these Government or WHO policy documents is the place of some of the more controversial aspects of end-of-life care, such as assistance in dying, physician-assisted suicide or euthanasia. Yet, as can be seen from the discussions in *Chapters 3 and 5*, there is a growing movement both within and without Government to provide some legal or policy infrastructure for activities that are undoubtedly occurring, either legally or illegally. This covert culture can be extremely damaging for recruitment and retention of staff. Knowledge and awareness of clandestine activities places stress on healthcare practitioners, yet an inability to provide assistance in dying when patients seek it can also be extremely harrowing (Schwarz, 2003). As Tuten (2001, p.64) observed, 'We teach what is right but practise what is legal. And we are disturbed when what is legal is not right.'

## The need for education as a policy initiative

Education has been identified as one of three planks in any national cancer pain relief programme, the other two being drug availability and legislation (WHO, 1996). These three issues have also since been identified as central to any national palliative care policy (Bruera and Sweeney, 2002). However, if widespread attitudinal change is to occur, then education is necessary not only in addition to policy, but as an integral part of policy, as significant investment will be required to provide the desired level of professional and public opinion shift.

Education of health professionals will be an ongoing concern for governments in relation to palliative care. It will be necessary to invest significant funds in education until a critical mass of health professionals is aware of the need both to implement palliative care early in the diagnosis of life-threatening illnesses and to provide adequate pain relief and palliative care for all people at the end of life. In *Better Palliative Care for Older People* (2004c), the WHO recommends that policy and decision makers need to ensure that the training of healthcare professionals includes sufficient time devoted to palliative medicine and the care of older people and that professionals are supported to keep up to date. Health professionals themselves are identified as needing to ensure they are adequately trained in palliative care for older people, including symptom management, communication and care co-ordination. Health professionals also need to ensure that older people are regarded as individuals, and that their right to make decisions about their health and social care is respected, and that they receive the unbiased information they need without age discrimination. Given the findings from studies such as Costello's (2002) there is a need for significant education aimed at attitudinal change to achieve this last cultural shift.

In *Palliative Care: The Solid Facts*, a number of policy implications related to the education of health professionals are identified. Palliative care needs to be a core part of the training and continuing professional education of relevant healthcare professionals and sufficient palliative care specialists must be supported and made available to provide this education. At a local policy level, healthcare organisations need to invest in supporting healthcare professionals to keep up to date and to develop cultures and work practices that make the best use of their palliative care skills (WHO, 2004a). Education is also required to ensure that health professionals understand their legal and ethical obligations to patients who are seeking end-of-life care as opposed to continued interventionist treatment (Ackerman, 2000; Rushton and Sabatier, 2001; Michael, 2002)

Education of the public is a critical aspect of policy, so that they understand what is possible in terms of palliative and end-of-life care implementation. It is particularly important in countries with a significant voluntary sector who provide much end-of-life care, since a clear understanding of what is possible and what is available will enable volunteers to either deliver or access the best possible care.

It will also be important to have consistency of language between palliative and end-of-life care, as the two are still used somewhat loosely and interchangeably in many policy documents. If palliative care is to begin at diagnosis, that is a very new concept for the general public, who tend to equate palliative care with hospice care, and may misunderstand their prognosis if the term is used without clarification. Policy and decision makers need to provide information to the public about the range of services available, including symptom control, and their effectiveness for older people facing life-threatening, chronic or progressive illnesses (WHO, 2004c).

Public education can be offered in a variety of media. Schools education has been extremely successful in acquainting young people with the work of hospices, for example, and schools also offer support programmes for children who are recently bereaved (WHO, 2004a). Books, plays and television programmes can also heighten awareness of the need for and importance of palliative and end-of-life care. The play '*Wit*' and the US television series '*On our own terms*', both chronicling end-of-life experiences in highly accessible and moving ways, were extremely successful in raising public awareness about end-of-life issues and what is desirable and possible in end-of-life care (Blacksher and Christopher, 2002). Bringing positive experiences of dying people and their families into the public domain is also a valuable strategy for raising awareness (obviously with appropriate consent) (WHO, 2004a). Other valuable strategies for raising awareness and for educating the public include Government support for self-help groups, first-hand education about available resources for patients and their families by health professionals at diagnosis; and more traditional public health strategies such as posters, leaflets and web-based information (NICE, 2004).

## Community involvement

In addition to community education, there is a strong move to involve the public in agenda setting in health policy in order to develop clearer communication strategies about what patients and carers want and what health services are realistically able to deliver. Community–state partnerships have been demonstrated to be extremely effective in driving health policy and legislative reform (Blacksher and Christopher, 2002). Involvement of the public has also on occasions resulted in significant financial gains through the interventions of charitable donors (Byock, 2001). Cancer networks in England and Wales should implement partnership groups that involve patients, carers and practitioners, and that the views of these groups should be taken into account when services are planned (NICE, 2004). It will be necessary to provide funding for education and support of partnership group members to ensure that they are properly skilled to participate in agenda setting. Failure to empower and educate the community to contribute to healthcare debate would only result in alienation and division between professionals and consumers, whereas strong community partnerships facilitate growth in end-of-life care services and build strong political alliances (Christopher, 2003).

Community engagement has four goals: to gather information, to educate individuals, to build community, and to reform policy, and 'collecting the stories and views of ordinary citizens and mining these views for underpinning values helps reformers move in the right direction and provides a basis for improving standards, practices and policies' (Blacksher and Christopher, 2002, p.16). There is a strong consumer movement emerging to involve the elderly in particular in making decisions about the types and mix of services they want to be available at the end of life and after bereavement (WHO, 2004c; EURAG, 2004). It is suggested that this is because 'baby-boomers', an age cohort well used to having a sense of control over their lives, are now choosing to exercise the same control over their deaths as they are ageing (Blacksher and Christopher, 2002).

## Future research directions

There is a clear need for increased research into end-of-life care. The UK spends only 0.18% of its total Government and charitable funding for cancer research on palliative and end-of-life care. The USA spends only 0.9% of its cancer research budget on palliative care (WHO, 2004a). The NICE Guidance (2004) identifies no less than 26 broad aspects of palliative and end-of-life care that are in need of research. In addition, the National Cancer Research Institute (NCRI)

Box 6.2 Key findings of National Cancer Research Institute review of supportive and palliative care research

- Lot of research evidence on needs, and on problems when care is not effective, but evidence on effective solutions is very patchy.
- Some research evidence comparing the importance of supportive and palliative care for patients with other health priorities.
- Interventions are often poorly defined and therefore difficult to replicate. Services often developed without evaluation; lack of comparative studies.
- Study populations are often highly selected, with a lack of acknowledgement of the time course of the disease. Lack of studies on elderly and different cultural groups.
- Outcome measures are extremely varied and are rarely collected in a systematic way.
- Need for:
    Longitudinal studies of preference and experience;
    Development and testing of different models and solutions;
    Comparisons with current best practice;
    Definitions of interventions, populations and outcomes;
    Outcome measures of complex interventions for use in clinical practice.
- Communication skills research is an area of success.
- Information delivery research needs methodology development.
- Major need for rigorous intervention studies carried out by multidisciplinary research teams.
- Need for research into symptoms other than pain.

From National Cancer Research Institute, 2004, p25

has provided a valuable overview of research into supportive and palliative care in the UK, the key points of which are highlighted in *Box 6.2*.

Research studies also require Government funding, particularly for major longitudinal studies. Research also requires a Government commitment to data infrastructure, such as core data sets that would allow links between different care settings in order to monitor patient needs and benchmark care delivery (WHO, 2004a). The need to benchmark requires a Government commitment to foster collaborative research, both between countries and between facilities and specialties. Such collaboration also assists with the dissemination of research findings and best available evidence (WHO, 2004c). Furthermore, those funding research should monitor the proportion of funds in any disease area directed towards palliative and end-of-life care, and invest in research to redress the balance.

Research into end-of-life care is not without its critics, as there are concerns that, for clinician investigators, the research aims may override the requirement to provide the best end-of-life care in order to maintain strict research treatment protocols. For patients, the concerns are that the dying patient may harbour the misconception that the research protocol provides the possibility of new hope, even cure (Williams and Haywood Jnr, 2003). Other researchers have expressed ethical concerns about the role of the participant observer when researching the experiences of the dying, and also concerns about the validity of consent when the person who originally gave the consent no longer has capacity (Lawton, 2001).

However, others argue that many dying patients still value autonomy, spiritual guidance, symptom relief and family support while wishing to contribute to the 'greater good' by being involved in end-of-life research. Further it is suggested that in conducting end-of-life research it is necessary to obtain consent from family members as well as the patient, as the experience of death is not confined to the dying person (Jubb, 2002). A number of strategies are available to address the tensions between researcher and clinician. These include: modifying the informed consent discussion for terminally ill participants in research; building a palliative care component into clinical trials; attending to the needs of the family as well as the research subject; pre-arranging for continuity of care so that dropping out of the trial will not affect the patient's access to medical care; providing education for investigators in end-of-life care and developing counselling strategies for terminally ill patients who are participating in research (Agrawal and Danis, 2002). Four values can be seen to be in tension for the clinician investigator: curative intent, palliative intent, and research and fiduciary obligations. Being open to the concerns of other members of the healthcare team is a valuable way for clinician investigators to become aware of conflicts between these values if they are finding it personally difficult to separate them (Williams and Haywood Jnr, 2003).

Despite the acknowledged difficulties in conducting research with the terminally ill, there are significant benefits to be gained from an evidence-based approach to end-of-life care. There are still many aspects of symptom control that little is known about, but which have a high prevalence in patients with terminal illness. Research into the best ways of managing these symptoms could provide significant relief for patients and their families at the end of life. These symptoms include anxiety (24–32% prevalence), confusion (5–38%), constipation (25–86%), depression (18–36%), dyspnoea (20–69%), fatigue (7–88%), incontinence (18–51%), loss of appetite (38–66%), nausea and vomiting (16–54%), [loss of?] sleep (19–88%), and weakness (35–100%) (Jubb, 2002).

The NICE Guidance is set out so that each section examines what research is needed to improve the evidence base around that particular aspect of end-of-life care. Twenty-six areas in all are identified where research is needed, and there are even specific recommendations about the type of research required, for example empirical or evaluative research. A number of the areas of research need relate to determining the most cost-effective ways to deliver services, for example, exchanging information, such as decision aids and innovative technology; providing general and specialist palliative care to patients out of hours; providing different models of family support; and providing and sustaining continuing education to GPs, district nurses, and hospital and home care staff.

Areas of evaluative research are highlighted to address the best way of delivering a particular service. For example, research is recommended into the best ways to provide multidisciplinary collaboration between generalist and specialist palliative care; spiritual support for different patient groups in different settings and at different stages of disease; safety and efficacy of complementary therapies; delivery of information about complementary therapies; effective co-ordination between social and healthcare services; effective maintenance of professional communication skills over time; effective psychotherapeutic interventions; and user participation in the delivery of supportive and palliative care in differing circumstances.

Empirical research is suggested to undertake mapping exercises. For example, there is a need to map patients' motivations, expectations and experiences of care in a range of contexts, to identify different services and patterns of care received and to identify ways to improve local service co-ordination. Mapping of carer pathways, identifying views about different services and patterns of care received and how services can best meet needs are other research priorities. Comparative studies are also needed to test different models of bereavement support; utility of bereavement support for different groups; which models of rehabilitation are most effective for different groups; differing models of palliative care services, including issues such as skill mix; methods of working; and mix of services. The role and contributions of respite care, allied health professionals and social workers are also identified as requiring investigation (NICE, 2004).

This (abbreviated) list gives some indication of the potential scope for research into palliative and end-of-life care. If, as has been suggested, end-of-life care is treated in the future as a public health issue, the scope for epidemiological research will increase significantly. There is also a need for dissemination of information about measurement tools for end-of-life research.

Notably there are no recommendations in the NICE Guidance for research into the legal and ethical issues surrounding end-of-life care, yet the debate continues in the health law and ethics literature. There seems to be a need to quantify and/or describe every aspect of end-of-life care except those related to the more difficult and controversial aspects of end-of-life care, both legal and illegal. These aspects include topics such as the development and use of advance directives; forgoing life-sustaining medical treatment, in particular artificial

## Box 6.3 Research recommendations to inform decisions about assistance in dying

*Patient views*

■ How do views change along the disease journey?

■ Do physical symptoms and psychological symptoms differ in their influence on a patient's wish for death?

■ How do different social, cultural and religious backgrounds affect a person facing the end of his or her life?

■ How do views change once patients have received palliative care, as opposed to being told about it?

*Carer views*

■ How do carers' views influence patients' views?

■ How do these views change during the course of an illness?

■ How does the availability of supporting services influence the views of carers?

*Professional views*

■ A more accurate understanding of the actions and intentions of doctors who state that they have ended a patient's life.

■ An understanding of the consequences of requiring doctors to offer and then bring about the ending of a patient's life.

■ An understanding of the impact on other healthcare professionals who would be involved in patient-assisted death. The Bill places a very heavy onus on doctors, as opposed to other professionals. Is it right that doctors should shoulder so much of the responsibility in relation to this issue?

*The general public*

■ How will permitting assisted dying affect society's view of the sick, frail and elderly?

*Experience in other countries*

■ To what extent can experience and research in other countries, both where patient-assisted death is legal and where it is not, inform our understanding of the impact that patient-assisted death would have in the UK?

*Practical implementation*

■ How would patient-assisted death be introduced into UK practice?

■ How would patient-assisted death safeguards be consistent or compatible with current practice?

■ What lessons can be drawn from other jurisdictions?

From NCHSPCS, 2004, website

nutrition and hydration; and requests for assistance in dying, physician-assisted suicide and even euthanasia. Yet opinion polls tell us that such practices exist (Hemmings, 2003), and there are lobby groups who both support and condemn the legalisation of physician-assisted suicide and assistance in dying, as discussed in *Chapter 3*, meaning that the debate is alive in the minds of the public. Health professional organisations have provided carefully considered professional and legal advice on forgoing life-sustaining treatment (General Medical Council, 2002) and decisions not to attempt cardiopulmonary resuscitation (BMA, RC [UK] and RCN, 2003). Yet none of the research recommendations made by the NCRI or NICE canvass these issues.

However, in the submission to the House of Lords Select Committee on the Assisted Dying for the Terminally Ill Bill 2004, the NCHSPCS identifies a comprehensive list of research topics relating to assistance in dying. The argument of NCHSPCS is that no legislation ought to be passed in relation to assistance in dying until these research questions have been answered. Although NCHSPCS is keen to point out that the list is not exhaustive, it is certainly a much more considered and comprehensive list of issues than has been previously collated, and is reproduced in full in *Box 6.3*.

From a policy perspective, it is clear that such an extensive research programme would require significant Government funding, requiring as it does some major population studies to ascertain with any confidence the answers to some of these questions. Notwithstanding this caveat, the identification of research topics in relation to assistance in dying by a major national organisation is an extremely positive step in coming to grips with the issue.

## Evaluation

Evaluation is the pivot of the range of recommendations made in relation to policy development and implementation, education, consumer involvement and research. Without evaluation on the success or otherwise of any of the strategies outlined in this chapter, the quality feedback loop is incomplete and the potential for improvement change is completely random. The WHO (2004c) recommends that policy and decision makers need to undertake at national or regional level, a 'quality audit' of palliative care services across all service delivery sites, and determine a tracking mechanism for improvements. The WHO further recommends that policy and decision makers invest in audit and quality improvement mechanisms across all palliative and end-of-life care service providers.

The PDSA cycle was described earlier as a quality activity, but evaluation requires determination of what is to be audited and how quality is to be measured. Evaluation can occur around patient outcomes, staff outcomes, management outcomes and infrastructure outcomes, such as evaluation of legislation or a national programme either relating to the totality of end-of-life care or specific elements within such a programme.

At patient level, benchmarking against other care providers offers an avenue for both research and evaluation. Variance analysis has been used in Wales (Fowell *et al*, 2002) to benchmark against the end-of-life best practice requirements of the integrated care pathway (LCP) developed in Liverpool (Ellershaw, 2001). Other evaluation studies may choose to focus on only one or two outcomes to evaluate the effectiveness of care, such as caregiver communication and patient feedback (Childress, 2001). Domains of quality at the patient level for end-of-life care identified for managed care pathways include: physical and emotional symptoms; support of function and autonomy; advance care planning; aggressive care near death; site of death, cardiopulmonary resuscitation; patient and family satisfaction; global quality of life; family burden; survival time; provider continuity and skill; and bereavement (Byock, 2001). It would appear that some of these domains are negative indicators of quality, and the expectation would be that they were not present on audit. Nonetheless, the checklist provides a useful overview of the components of evaluation and is of note because it includes some of the (for the UK) more controversial issues such as advance directives and cardiopulmonary resuscitation.

At the staff and management outcomes level, a national hospice quality improvement programme in the US divided outcome measures identified by the hospices into three main groups: utilisation outcomes, instrumental outcomes and end results outcomes. Utilisation outcomes included items such as admissions as percentage of referrals, potential volunteers screened, staff performance reviews, and building inspections. Instrumental outcomes included items such as cost per admission or patient day, satisfaction of discharge planners, staff education, and fundraising. End result outcomes included competent staff, staff satisfaction, leadership and volunteer satisfaction (D'Onofrio, 2001).

At a regional level, end-of-life care programmes can be evaluated in a variety of ways. An evaluation of a palliative care programme across the Edmonton region used two outcome indicators, access to palliative care consultations and place of death, to evaluate the success of the implementation of the programme (Bruera and Sweeney, 2002). In 1990 the WHO identified the three planks of any national programme for cancer control: education, opioid availability and policy or legislative framework. More recently, the WHO has produced a tool for governments to evaluate and benchmark their success in making opioids widely available for use in pain management, by developing a set of guidelines for self-assessment (2000).

---

**Box 6.4 Elements required to secure adequate and appropriate end-of-life care legislation**

■ Does the legislation provide for adequate and appropriate training of healthcare personnel in pain management and palliative care?

■ Does the legislation recognise the significant ethical dilemmas presented by assisted suicide and adequately support medical personnel in their attempts to resolve these dilemmas? Does the legislation incorporate public opinion regarding assisted suicide?

■ Does the legislation assure that healthcare facilities and personnel will consistently adhere to patients' advance directives? Are healthcare consumers and family member/caregivers adequately educated and supported in the development of advance directives?

■ Does the legislation support evidence-based practice to secure appropriate and timely delivery of care? Does the legislation recognise innovation and encourage best practice efforts?

■ Are factors attributed to the under-utilisation of hospice services adequately addressed?

■ Does the legislation encourage the development of communication skills specific to death and dying?

■ Does the legislation provide a vehicle for addressing the psychosocial aspects of death and dying?

■ Are specific attempts made to adequately and appropriately address the current level of under-treated pain and symptom management?

■ Does the legislation address the current reimbursement barriers regarding pain and symptom management, palliative care and hospice services?

■ Does the legislation take authority away from existing state legislation or are the efforts designed to supplement current state mandate?

■ Does the legislation provide for public education efforts regarding end-of-life options?

■ Are the appropriations provided adequate to address the key issues?

From Roff, 2001, p.58

---

The evaluation of the effectiveness of legislation underpinning end-of-life care is a complex process, and Roff (2001) suggests a series of questions that are set out in *Box 6.4*. Although Roff refers only to legislation in her checklist, many of the provisions identified could be better managed through a policy framework, which is less cumbersome to amend as evaluation provides feedback about best practice. It is always tempting to imagine that enshrining all requirements for practice in legislation is the best way of ensuring that changes will occur. However, one of the difficulties in developing comprehensive legislation is that the process of introducing legislation through Parliament is often lengthy and onerous, and making future changes will be equally so. Often it is better to use the legislation as a framework with provision to make relevant regulations and to fill in the detail either through regulations or through policy. In addition, several of the issues that Roff has identified to be enshrined in legislation in reality relate to good healthcare practices, and are perhaps better managed through improved education and surveillance of practice, rather than through any statutory provisions.

Much of the above evaluation framework could usefully be applied to local policy as well as national legislation, as it addresses both clinical and management aspects of end-of-life care. However, what is ultimately of importance is that outcome measures are determined, evaluation against those measures is undertaken, feedback from the evaluation is provided and improvement strategies implemented where appropriate.

## Conclusion

This final chapter has examined future directions for policy and research. It has examined policy development and implementation, and inter-related these to education, community involvement and research. Central to each of these topics is evaluation, and a model has been proposed which identifies the role of each in informing and shaping the others. It is clear that end-of-life care is an area in need of strong policy development and research, and in the past five years in particular many recommendations have been made in relation to policy, education, consumer involvement, evaluation and research. These recommendations have been assembled and considered within this final chapter.

The purpose of this book has been to provide a review of policy on palliative care and end-of-life care, focusing specifically on the UK and the USA. The purpose was to provide a background document against which to focus the work of the newly established Centre to Improve Research, Education and Practice in Palliative and End-of-Life Care at the University of Nottingham, UK. It has focused on past and current policy, and has also explored a number of major issues, which have included: the ongoing or continuing legal and ethical debates around end-of-life care; considerations around clinical practice from a range of stakeholder perspectives; and the major lobby groups at both national and international level who are both leading and influencing the debates. In addition, the book examined international trends in policy development, prior to concluding with this chapter on future directions for policy and research.

# References

Academy of Medical Royal Colleges (2004) *Assisted Dying for the Terminally Ill Bill: Submission to the House of Lords Select Committee*. London: Royal College of Physicians.

Ackermann RJ (2000) Withholding and withdrawing life-sustaining treatment. *Amer Fam Phys* **62**(7): 1555.

Ackroyd R (2003) Advance directives – the ethical pros and cons. *Eur J Pall Care* **10**(3): 116–18.

Addington-Hall J (1998) *Dying in the NHS: Seminar Promoted by the Nuffield Trust*. Oxford: Nuffield Trust.

Agrawal M, Danis M (2002) End-of-Life care for terminally ill patients in clinical research. *J Pall Med* **5**(5): 729–37.

Allen F (2002) Where are the women in end-of-life research? *Behav Change* **19**(1): 39–51.

Allen RS, Kwak J, Lokken K, Haley WE (2003) End-of-life issues in the context of Alzheimer's disease. *Alzheimer's Care Q* **4**: 312–30.

American Academy of Paediatrics (1994) Guidelines on forgoing life-sustaining medical treatment. *Pediatrics* **93**: 532–6.

American Medical Association (1999) Medical futility in end-of-life care: Report of the Council on Ethical and Judicial Affairs. *J Am Med Assoc* **281**: 937–41.

Annas GJ (2005) "Culture of Life" politics at the bedside – The case of Terri Schiavo. *N Engl J Med* **352**(16): 1710–15.

Anonymous (2003) First State-by-State "Report Card" on care for the dying finds mediocre care nationwide. *J Hospice Pall Care Nurs* **5**(1): 14–18.

Australian Medical Association (1997) *Care of Severely and Terminally Ill Patients*. Sydney: Australian Medical Association.

Barclay S (1998) How might care for the dying be improved in general practice? In *Dying in the NHS: Seminar promoted by the Nuffield Trust*. Oxford: Nuffield Trust.

Batehup L (2003) Letter: Pathway can provide quality care for the dying. *Nurs T* **99**(31): 14–15.

Berger JT (2004) Letters: Advance directives, due process and medical futility: Response to Fine and Mayo. *Ann Inter Med* **140**(5): 402–3.

Bix B (1995) Physician assisted suicide and the United States Constitution. *Mod Law Rev* **58**(3): 404–11.

Blacksher E, Christopher M (2002) On the road to reform: Advocacy and activism in end-of-life care. *J Pall Med* **5**(1): 13–22.

Blasi ZV, Hurley AC, Volicer L (2002) End-of-life care in dementia: A review of problems, prospects and solutions in practice. *J Amer Directors Assoc* 3: 57–65.

British Medical Association (1995) *Advance Statements about Medical Treatment. Code of Practice with Explanatory Notes*. London: BMJ Publishing Group.

British Medical Association (1998) *Withholding and Withdrawing Life-Prolonging Treatment: Guidance for Decision-Making*. London: British Medical Association.

British Medical Association and the Law Society (2002) *Assessment of Mental Capacity: Guidance for Doctors and Lawyers*. 2nd edn. London: BMA.

British Medical Association, Resuscitation Council, and Royal College of Nursing (2003) *Decisions Relating to Cardiopulmonary Resuscitation*. London: BMA.

Brown M (2002) Participating in end of life decisions: The role of general practitioners (GPs). *Aust Fam Phys* **31**(1): 60–2.

Bruera E, Sweeney C (2002) Palliative care models: International perspective. *J Pall Med* **5**(2): 319–27.

Burt RA (2000) The limitations of protocols for end-of-life care. *Respir Care* **45**(12) 1523–9.

Byock IR (2001 End-of-life care: A public health crisis and an opportunity for managed care. *Amer J Manag Care* **7**(12): 1123–32.

Campbell ML (2002) End-of-life care in the ICU: Current practices and future hopes. *Crit Care Nurs Clin N Amer* **14**: 197–200.

Carter B (2003) Legal issues at end of life: A Guardian's perspective. *Chisholm Health Ethics Bull* **8**(3): 4–6.

Cartwright C (2000) End-of-life decision making: Practical and ethical issues for health professionals. *Australas J Ageing* **19**(2): 57–62.

Castledine G (2004) Nurses should be more involved in DNR decisions. *Brit J Nurs* **13**(3): 3.

Charatan F (2005a) President Bush and Congress intervene in "right to die" case. *Br Med J* **330**(7493): 687.

Charatan F (2005b) Autopsy supports claim that Schiavo was in a persistent vegetative state. *Br Med J* **330**(7506): 1467.

Chiarella M (1995a) Nursing records: Their roles in court. *ACORN Journal* **8**(1): 29–30.

Chiarella M (1995b) Voluntary euthanasia: Update on legislation. *ACORN Journal* **8**(3) 22–5.

Chiarella M (2000) Extending life. In J Lumby, D Picone (Eds). *Clinical Challenges: Focus on Nursing*. Sydney: Allen & Unwin.

Chief Rabbi (2003) *Patient (Assisted Dying) Bill Something Jewish, 04.06.03*. [accessed 21 October 2004]. From http://www.somethingjewish.co.uk/articles/205_patient_assisted_dyi.htm

Childress SB (2001) Enhance end of life. *Nurs Manag* **32**(10): 32–5.

Christopher MJ (2003) A future vision of innovative and expanded community partnerships in end-of-life care. *Home Health Care Manag Pract* **15**(2): 105–9.

Cohen-Almagor R (2002) Dutch perspectives on palliative care in the Netherlands. *Issues in Law and Med* **18**(2): 111–26.

Colloquium of the Royal Netherlands Academy of Arts and Sciences (1999) *Epidemiological and Clinical Aspects of End-of-Life Decision-Making*. Amsterdam, 7–9 October.

Committee on Medical Ethics (2000) *The Impact of the Human Rights Act (1998) on Medical Decision Making*. London: British Medical Association.

Costello J (2002) Do not resuscitate orders and older patients: Findings from an ethnographic study of hospital wards for older people. *J Adv Nurs* **39**(5): 491–9.

Counsell C, Adorno G, Guin P (2003) Establishing an end-of-life program in an academic acute care hospital. *Spinal Cord Injury Nurs* **20**(4): 238–49.

Csikai EL, Bass K (2000) Health care social workers' views on ethical issues, practice and policy in end-of-life care. *Soc Work in Health Care* **32**(2): 1–22.

Daher M, Tabri H, Stjernsward J, Ammar W, Nabhan T, Abounasr K, Micheline B, Dakwar A, Khoury M, Lteif A, Stephan E, Tueni E, Makarem S, Ferris FD, Kanazi Ghassan T, Samia G, Naja Z, Mansour Z (2002) Lebanon: Pain relief and palliative care. *J Pain Symptom Manag* **24**(2): 200–4.

Dahl JL (2002) Working with regulators to improve the standard of care in pain management: The US experience. *J Pain Sympt Manag* **24**(2): 136–47.

Davaasuren O (2002) Mongolia: The present situation and future of palliative care. *J Pain Sympt Manag* **24**(2): 208–10.

Department for Constitutional Affairs (2002a) *Making Decisions: Helping People who Have Difficulty Deciding for Themselves*. London: Lord Chancellor's Department.

Department for Constitutional Affairs (2002b) *Making Decisions. Leaflet 2. Helping People who Have Difficulty Deciding for Themselves: A Guide for Health Care Professionals*. London: Lord Chancellor's Department.

Department for Constitutional Affairs (2002c) *Making Decisions. Leaflet 4. Helping People who Have Difficulty Deciding for Themselves: A Guide for Legal Professionals*. London: Lord Chancellor's Department.

Department of Health (1999) *A Policy Framework for Commissioning Cancer Services: Report to the CMOs for England and Wales (The Calman-Hine Report)*. London: Stationery Office.

Department of Health (2000) *The NHS Cancer Plan*. London: Stationery Office.

Diggory P, Judd M (2000) Advance directives: Questionnaire survey of NHS Trusts. *Br Med J* **320**: 24–5.

Dimond B (2000) The legal aspects of living wills: A need for clarity. *Int J Pall Nurs* **6**(6): 304–6

Dimond B (2001) Legal aspects of consent 15: Living wills and the common law. *Br J Nurs* **10**(19): 1256–7.

Disability Rights Commission (2004) *Health and Independent Living Disability Rights Commission* [accessed 21 October 2004]. From http://www.drc-gb.org/publicationsandreports/campaigndetails.asp?section=he&id=324

D'Onofrio CN (2001) Hospice Quality Improvement Programs: An initial examination. *J Nurs Care Q* **15**(4): 29–47.

Doukas DJ, Hardwig J (2003) Using the family covenant in planning end of life care; obligation and promises of patients, families and physicians. *J Amer Geriatr Soc* **51**: 1155–8.

Doyle DL, Hanks GWC, MacDonald N (1998) *Oxford Textbook of Palliative Care Medicine* (2nd edn). Oxford: Oxford University Press.

Dworkin R (1993) *Life's Dominion. An Argument About Abortion and Euthanasia*. London: Harper Collins.

Dyer C (2004a) London hospital to face High Court for allegedly refusing to resuscitate disabled girl. *Br Med J* **328**: 125.

Dyer C (2004b) Patient challenges GMC guidance on withdrawing treatment. *Br Med J* **328**: 541.

Dyer C (2004c) GMC appeals against judgment on withholding treatment. *Br Med J* **329**: 818.

Edmonds P (1998) How might care for dying people be improved in general hospitals. In *Dying in the NHS: Seminar Promoted by the Nuffield Trust*. Oxford: Nuffield Trust.

Edmonds P, Rogers A (2003) "If only someone had told me..." A review of patients dying in hospital. *Clin Med* **3**: 149–52.

Ellershaw J (2001) Care of the dying: Clinical pathways: An innovation to disseminate clinical excellence. *Innovations in End-of-life Care* **3**(4). From: www.edc.org/lastacts

Ellershaw J, Murphy D (2003) The national pathway network of palliative care pathways. *J Integrated Care Pathways* **7**: 11–13.

Ellershaw J, Ward C (2003) Care of the dying patient: The last hours of life. *Br Med J* **326**: 30–34.

EURAG, European Federation of Older Persons (2004) *Making Palliative Care a Priority Topic on the European Health Agenda and Recommendations for the Development of Palliative Care in Europe.* Graz: Austria: EURAG.

Expert Advisory Group on Cancer (1995) *A Policy Framework for Commissioning Cancer Services: Report to the CMOs of England and Wales.* London: Department of Health.

Ferris FD, Bowen K, Farley J, Hardwick M, Lamontagne C, Lundy M, Syme A, West PJ (2002) A model to guide patient and family care based on nationally accepted principles and norms of practice. *J Pain Sympt Manag* **24**(2): 106–23.

Fine RL, Mayo TW (2003) Resolution of futility by due process: Early experience with the Texas Advance Directives Act. *Ann Inter Med* **138**(8): 743–6.

Finucane TE (2004) Letters: Advance directives, due process and medical futility: Response to Fine and Mayo. *Ann Inter Med* **140**(5): 402–3.

Flamm AL, Smith ML (2004) Advance directives, due process and medical futility. *Ann Inter Med* **140**(5): 403–4.

Ford N (2002) Treatment at the end of life and ethics. *Chisholm Health Ethics Bulletin* **Summer**: 3–6.

Fowell A, Finlay I, Johnstone R, Minto L (2002) An integrated care pathway for the last two days of life. Wales-wide benchmarking in palliative care. *Int J Pall Nurs* **8**(12): 566–73.

Frith M (2004a) We just want a little more time with Charlotte. *The Independent*, **2 October**: 21.

Frith M (2004b) Court to decide fate of sick baby despite mother's appeal. *The Independent* **14 October**: 15.

General Medical Council, UK (2002) *Withholding and Withdrawing Life-Prolonging Treatments: Good Practice in Decision-Making.* London: GMC (UK).

Gillick MR (2004) Advance care planning. *New Engl J Med* **350**(1): 7–8.

Glare PA, Tobin B (2002) End-of-life issues: Case 2. *Med J Aust* **176**: 80–1.

Glare P, Virik K (2001) Can we do better in end-of-life care? The mixed management model and palliative care. *Med J Aust* **175**: 530–3.

Goldberg S (2002) Do-not-resuscitate orders in the OR – suspend or enforce? *AORN J* **76**(2): 296–9.

Gomez-Batiste X, Porta J, Tuca A, Corrales E, Madrid F, Trelis J, Fontanals D, Borras JM, Stjernsward J, Salva A, Rius E (2002) Spain: The WHO Demonstration Project of Palliative Care Implementation in Catalonia: Results at 10 years (1991–2001). *J Pain Sympt Manage* **24**(2): 239–44.

Gordon NP, Shade SB (1999) Advance Directives are more likely among seniors asked about end-of-life preferences. *Arch Intern Med* **159**(7): 701–4.

Gostin L (2005) Ethics, the constitution, and the dying process: The case of Theresa Marie Schiavo. *J Am Med Assoc* **293**(19): 2403–7.

Hastings Center (1987) *Guidelines on the Termination of Life-Sustaining Treatment and the Care of the Dying*. Bloomington and Indianapolis: Hastings Center.

Hemmings P (2003) Dying wishes. *Nurs Times* **99**(47): 20–2.

Higginson IJ, Constantini M (2002) Communication in end-of-life cancer care: A comparison of team assessments in three European countries. *J Clin Oncol* **20**(17): 3674–82.

Higginson IJ, Sen-Gupta GJA (2000) Place of care in advanced cancer: A qualitative systematic literature review of patient preference. *J Pall Med* **3**: 287–300.

Higgs R (1999) The diagnosis of dying. *J R Coll Phys Lond* **33**: 110–2.

Hinton J (1994) Can home care maintain an acceptable quality of life for patients with terminal cancer and their relatives? *Pall Med* **8**: 183–96.

Hospice Education Institute (Undated) A short history from the Middle Ages to the 21st Century [Accessed 6 October 2004]. From http://www. hospiceworld.org/history.htm

House of Lords Select Committee (2005) *Assisted Dying for the Terminally Ill Bill – First Report*. Available from http://www.publications.parliament. uk/pa/ld200405/ldselect/ldasdy/86/8602.htm

International Task Force on Euthanasia and Assisted Suicide (2002) Ohio House OKs Bill against assisted suicide. *Update* **16**(2).

IOM Committee on Care at the End of Life (1997) *Approaching Death: Improving Care at the End of Life*. Washington DC: National Academy Press.

Johnston G, Burge F (2002) Analytic framework for clinician provision of end-of-life care. *J Pall Care* **18**(3): 141–9.

Jolly M, Cornock M (2003) Application of the doctrine of double effect in end stage disease. *Int J Pall Nurs* **9**(6): 240–4.

Jones RG (2001) Ethical and legal issues in the care of people with dementia. *Rev Clin Gerontol* **11**: 245–68.

Jubb AM (2002) Palliative care research: Trading ethics for an evidence base. *J Med Ethics* **28**(6): 342–6.

Kaasa S, Breivik H, Jordhoy M (2002) Norway: Development of palliative care. *J Pain Sympt Manag* **24**(2): 211–14.

Kellehear A (2001) The changing face of dying in Australia. *Med J Aust* **175**: 508–10.

Kelly D (2003) A commentary on 'an integrated care pathway for the last two days of life'. *Int J Pall Nurs* **9**(1): 39.

Kennedy I (2001) *Bristol Royal Infirmary Inquiry. Learning from Bristol: The Report of the Public Inquiry into Children's Heart Surgery at the Bristol Royal Infirmary (1984–1995)*. Command Paper: CM 5207.

Kennedy I, Grubb A (2000) *Medical Law* (3rd edn). London: Butterworths.

Kohm LM, Brigner BN (1998) Women and assisted suicide: Exposing the gender vulnerability to acquiescent death. *Cardozo Women's Law Journal* **4**: 241.

Kubler-Ross E (1993) *On Death and Dying*. New York: Collier Books.

Kyba FC (2002) Legal and ethical issues in end-of-life care. *Crit Care Nurs Clin N Amer* **14**: 141–55.

Langley K, Nolan K, Nolan T, Norman C, Provost L (1996) *The Improvement Guide*. San Fransisco: Jossey-Bass.

Lawton J (2001) Pearls, pith and provocation – gaining and maintaining consent: Ethical concerns raised in a study of dying patients *Qualitative Health Res* **11**(5): 693–705.

Lee R (2004) *De-listing of Generic HIV Drugs Fuels Criticism of WHO.* [Accessed 3 December 2004] From Washingtonblade.com

Lee K, Buze K, Fustukian S (2001) *Health Policy in a Globalising World*. New York: Cambridge University Press.

Leonard CT, Doyle RL, Raffin TA (1999) Do not resuscitate orders in the face of patient and family opposition. *Crit Care Med* **27**: 1045–7.

Luce JM, Alpers A (2001) End-of-life care: What do the American courts say? *Crit Care Med* **29**(2): 40–5.

Luczak J, Kotlinska-Lemieszek A, Kluziak M, Bozewicz A (2002) Poland: Cancer pain and palliative care. *J Pain Sympt Manag* **24**(2): 215-21.

Lynn J, Adamson DM (2003) *Living Well at the End of Life: Adapting Health Care to Serious Chronic Illness in Old Age*. Arlington VA: Rand Health.

Lynn J, Gregory CO (2003) Editorial: Regulating hearts and minds: The mismatch of law, custom and resuscitation decisions. *J Amer Geriatr Soc* **51**: 1502–3.

Macleod R (2001) A national strategy for palliative care in New Zealand. *J Pall Med* **4**(1): 70–4.

Macleod R (2002) Doctors' anxieties in end-of-life care. *Curr Therapeutics* **October**: 57–59.

Mareiniss DP (2005) A comparison of Cruzan and Schiavo: The burden of proof, due process and autonomy on the persistently vegetative patient. *J Legal Med* **26**: 233–59.

Marie Curie (2004) Overview of Current Project – Liverpool Care Pathway for the Dying Patient – Making it Happen [Accessed 6 October 2004] From http://www.lcp-mariecurie.org.uk/about/

Masuda Y, Fetters MD, Hattori A, Mogi N, Naito M, Iguchi A, Uemura K (2003) Physician's report on the impact of living will at the end of life in Japan. *J Med Ethics* **29**(4): 248–52.

Mathew A, Cowley S, Bliss J, Thistlewood G (2003) The development of palliative care in national Government policy in England (1986–2000). *Pall Med* **17**: 270–82.

McPhee J, Stewart C (2005) Recent developments in law. *J Bioethical Inq* **2**(1): 5.

Meisel A, Snyder L, Quill T (2000) Seven legal barriers to end-of-life care. *JAMA* **284**: 2495–501.

Mendelson D (1999) End of life: Legal framework. In I Freckleton, K Petersen (Eds) *Controversies in Health Law*. Sydney: Federation Press.

Metropolitan Life Insurance Company (1999) *The Metlife Juggling Act Study: Balancing Caregiving with Work and the Costs Involved*. Westport CT: Metropolitan Life Insurance Company.

Michael JE (2002) DNR orders: Proceed with caution. *Nurs Manag* **33**(5): 22–3, 56.

Miller PJ (2000) Life after death with dignity: The Oregon experience. *Soc Work* **45**(3): 263–71.

Mongolian Society for Open Foundation. From http://www.soros.org.mn/show_events.php?what=detial&EID=89

Moody J (2003) Dementia and personhood: Implications for advance directives. *Nurs Older People* **15**(4): 18–21.

Mosoiu D (2002) Romania 2002: Cancer pain and palliative care. *J Pain Sympt Manag* **24**(2): 225–7.

National Cancer Research Institute (2004) *Supportive and Palliative Research in the UK: Report of the NCRI Strategic Planning Group on Supportive and Palliative Care*. London: NCRI.

National Council for Hospice and Specialist Palliative Care Services (2001) *Building on Success: Strategic Agenda for 2001 to 2004*. London: NCHSPCS.

National Council for Hospice and Specialist Palliative Care Services (2004) *Submission on the Assisted Dying for the Terminally Ill Bill*. London: NCHSPCS.

National Hospice and Palliative Care Organisation (Undated) History of hospice care [Accessed 6 October, 2004] From http://www.nhpco.org/i4a/pages/index.cfm?pageid=3285

National Institute for Clinical Excellence (2004) *Guidance on Cancer Services: Improving Supportive and Palliative Care for Adults with Cancer. The Manual*. London: NICE.

Neeley GS (1994) The constitutional right to suicide, the quality of life and the 'slippery slope': An explicit reply to lingering concerns. *28 Akron Law Review:* 53.

New South Wales Health Department (2004) *Using Advanced Care Directives: New South Wales*. Sydney: New South Wales Health Department.

New South Wales Health Department (2005) *Guidelines for End-of-Life Care and Decision-Making*. Sydney: New South Wales Health Department.

NHS Modernisation Agency Cancer Services Collaborative: Palliative Care (2004) [Accessed 5 October 2004) From http://www.modern.nhs.uk/scripts/default.asp?site_id=26&id=12771

Nolde D (2003/04) The New York State Health Care Proxy Law and the issue of artificial hydration and nutrition. *J New York State Nurses Assoc* **Fall/Winter**: 23–8.

Nursing and Midwifery Council (2002) *Code of Professional Conduct*. London: Nursing and Midwifery Council.

Office of the Attorney General, State of Maryland (2003) *Advance Directives: A Guide to Maryland Law on Health Care Decisions*. Baltimore: Office of the Attorney General.

Office for National Statistics (2002) *Annual Review of the Registrar General on Deaths in England and Wales 2000*. London: Office for National Statistics.

Oguz N, Yasemin M, Steven H, Buken N, Civaner M (2003) End-of-life care in Turkey. *Camb Q Health Care Ethics* **12**: 279–84.

Pain Society (2004a) *Opioid Medications for Persistent Pain: Information for Patients*. London: The Pain Society.

Pain Society (2004b) *Recommendations for the Appropriate Use of Opioids for Persistent Non-Cancer Pain*. London: The Pain Society.

Paterson M (2000 Dealing with life and death decisions. *Kai Tiaki Nursing NZ* **14–15**: 18.

Pearson A, Robertson-Malt S, Walsh K, Fitzgerald M (2001) Intensive care nurses' experience of caring for brain dead organ donor patients. *J Clin Nurs* **10**: 132–9.

Pooler J, McCrory F, Steadman Y, Westwell H, Peers S (2003) Dying at home: A care pathway for the last days of life in a community setting. *Int J Pall Nurs* **9**(6): 258–63.

Powell M (1999) UK introduces NHS "Oscars". *Br Med J* **318**: 612.

Price CA (2003) Resources for planning palliative and end-of-life care for patients with kidney disease. *Nephrol Nurs J* **30**(6): 649–64.

Putnam CE (2001) *New Information on Death with Dignity*. Hastings Centre Report 8.

Quill TE (2005) Terri Schiavo – a tragedy compounded. *N Engl J Med* **352**(16): 1630–33.

Quill TE, Byock IR (2000) Responding to intractable terminal suffering: The role of terminal sedation and voluntary refusal of food and fluids. ACP-ASIM End-of-Life Care Consensus Panel. American College of Physicians/American Society of Internal Medicine. *Ann Inter Med* **132**(5) 408–14

Quill TE, Cassel CK (2003) Professional organisations' position statements on physician-assisted suicide: A case for studied neutrality. *Ann Inter Med* **138**(3):208–11.

Quinlan O (2004) Advance directives: Uses and legal standing in England. *Geriatric Med* **34**(4): 19–20, 22.

Reb AM (2003) Palliative and end of life care: Policy analysis. *Oncol Nurs Forum* **30**(1): 35–50.

Rich BA (2002) The ethics of surrogate decision-making. *Western J Med* **176**(2): 127–9.

Roff S (2001) Analyzing end-of-life care legislation: A social work perspective. In GRA Weissman (Ed) *Behavioural and Social Sciences in 21st Century Health Care: Contributions and Opportunities*. New York: Haworth Social Work Practice Press.

Royal College of Nursing (2004) *Royal College of Nursing confirms opposition to Assisted Dying Bill and Calls for Improved Palliative Care RCN Media* [Accessed 21 October 2004]. From http://www.rcn.org.uk/news/display.php?ID=1255&area=Press

Royal College of Physicians Committee on Ethical Issues (2003) *Response to Patient (Assisted Dying) Bill Royal College of Physicians, 23 July 2003* [Accessed 21 October 2004]. From http://www.rcplondon.ac.uk/college/statements/padb_response.htm

Rushton CH, Sabatier KH (2001) The nursing leadership consortium on end-of-life care: The response of the nursing profession to the need for improvement in palliative care. *Nurs Outlook* **49**(1): 58–60.

Ryan B (2004) Legally speaking. Advance directives: Your role. *RN* 67(5): 59–60, 62

Saunders CM (ed) (1985) *The Management of Terminal Illness* (2nd edn). London: Edward Arnold.

Saunders P (2003) Patient (Assisted Dying) Bill – a dangerous document that Christian doctors should oppose. *Triple Helix* [accessed 21 October 2004]. From http://www.cmf.org.uk/helix/sum03/editor1.htm

Scanlon C (2003) Ethical concerns in end-of-life care. *Amer J Nurs* **103**(1): 48–56.

Schwarz JK (1999) Assisted dying and nursing practice. *Image: J Nurs Scholarship* **31**: 367–73.

Schwarz JK (2003) Understanding and responding to patients' requests for assistance in dying. *J Nurs Scholarship* **35**(4): 377–84.

Sepulveda C, Marlin A, Yoshida T, Ullrich A (2002) Palliative care: The World Health Organisation's global perspective. *J Pain Sympt Manag* **24**(2): 91–6.

Seskevicius A (2002) Lithuania: Status of cancer pain and palliative care. *J Pain Sympt Manag* **24**(2): 205–7.

Seymour J (2000) Negotiating natural death in intensive care. *Soc Sci Med* **51**: 1241–52.

Seymour J, Clark D, Marples R (2002) Palliative care and policy in England: A review of health improvement plans for 1999–2003. *Pall Med* **16**: 5–11.

Shah S, Lloyd-Williams M (2003) End-of-life decision-making – Have we got it right? *Eur J Cancer Care* **12**: 212–14.

Simpson M (2003) Developing education support for community nurses: Principles and practice of palliative care. *Nurs Manag* **9**(9): 9–12.

Smith J, Taylor A, Jones A (2003) Dear Editor – response to Kelly D's article. *Int J Pall Nurs* **9**(2): 86–7.

Solomon MZ (2001) *Factors Inhibiting Optimal End-of-Life Decision-Making in US Hospitals.* Paper presented at the 7th Congress of the European Association for Palliative Care 1–5 April, Palermo.

Stanley JM (ed) (1989) *Appleton Consensus: Suggested International Guidelines for Decisions to Forgo Medical Treatment.* Proceedings of Guidelines for Non-Treatment Decisions: An International Working Conference, 18–19 May 1988, Lawrence University, Appleton, Wisconsin, USA.

Stanley JM (ed) (1992) Appleton Consensus: Suggested International Guidelines for Decisions to Forgo Medical Treatment. *J Med Ethics* **18**(Suppl): 1–22.

Stjernsward J (2002) Uganda: Initiating a government health response to pain relief and palliative care. *J Pain Sympt Manag* **24**(2): 257–64

SUPPORT Principal Investigators (1995) A controlled trial to improve care for seriously ill hospitalised patients. *J Amer Med Assoc* **274**(20): 1591–8.

Takeda F (2002) Japan: Status of cancer pain and palliative care. *J Pain Sympt Manag* **24**(2): 197–9.

Taylor L (1997) Persistent vegetative state: The gap between law and medicine. *Br J Ther Rehab* **4**(12): 640–5.

Ten Have H, Clark D (eds) (2002) *The Ethics of Palliative Care: European Perspectives.* Philadelphia: Open University.

Travis S, Hunt P (2001a) Supportive and palliative care networks: A new model for integrated care. *Int J Pall Nurs* **7**(10): 501–4.

Travis S, Mason J, Mallett C, Laverty D (2001b) Guidelines in respect of advance directives: The position in England. *Int J Pall Nurs* **7**(10): 493–500.

Tuten M (2001) A death with dignity in Oregon. *Oncol Nurs Forum* **28**: 58–65.

Twenty-One Health Organisations and the United States Drug Enforcement Agency (2001) *Promoting Pain Relief and Preventing Abuse of Pain Medications: A Critical Balancing Act.* Washington DC: US Drug Enforcement Agency.

UK Clinical Ethics Network (2004) *Winston-Jones Decision Announced.* [Accessed 22 October 2004] from http://www.ethics-network.org.uk/new.htm

United Kingdom Parliament (2004) *Lords set up Select Committee on the Assisted Dying for the Terminally Ill Bill* [HL] [Accessed 21 October 2004]. From http://www.parliament.uk/parliamentary_committees/lords_press_notices/pnl14070assis

Ventafridda V (2002) Italy: Status of cancer pain and palliative care. *J Pain Sympt Manag* **24**(2): 194–6.

Volicer L, Cantor MD, Derse AR, Edwards DM, Prudhomme AD, Rasinski-Gregory DC, Reagan JE, Tulsky JA, Fox E (2002) Advance care planning by proxy for residents of long-term care facilities who lack decision-making capacity. *J Amer Geriatr Soc* **50**: 761–7.

Volker DL (2001) Perspectives on assisted dying: Oncology nurses' experiences with requests for assisted dying from terminally ill patients with cancer. *Oncol Nurs Forum* **28**(1): 39–49.

Watkins P (2003) Editorial: "The ceaseless pursuit of triumph over death in life". *Clin Med* **3**: 1.

Welsh Office (1996) *Cancer Services in Wales: A Report by the Cancer Services Expert Group*. Cardiff: Welsh Office.

Wenk R, Bertolino M (2002) Argentina: Palliative care status 2002. *J Pain Symp Manag* **24**(2): 166–9.

Williams G (2001) The doctrine of double effect and terminal sedation. *Med Law Rev* **9**(1): 41–53.

Williams MA, Haywood C Jnr (2003) Critical care research on patients with advance directives or do-not-resuscitate status: Ethical challenges for clinician investigators *Crit Care Med* **31**(Suppl 3): 167–71.

World Federation of Right to Die Societies (2004) *The Joint Committee of Human Rights' Response to the Patient (Assisted Dying) Bill World Federation of Right to Die Societies 2003* [Accessed 21 October 2004] From http://www.worldrtd.net/news/world/?id=582

World Health Organisation (1990) *Cancer Pain Relief and Palliative Care*, Technical report series 804. Geneva: WHO.

World Health Organisation (1996) *Cancer Pain Relief* (2nd edn) with a guide to opioid availability. Geneva: WHO.

World Health Organisation (2000) *Achieving Balance in National Opioids Control Policy: Guidelines for Assessment*. Geneva: WHO:

World Health Organisation (2003a) *Global Action Against Cancer*. Geneva: WHO.

World Health Organisation (2003b) *Palliative Care: Symptom Management and End-of-Life Care: Integrated Management of Adolescent and Adult Illness*. Geneva: WHO.

World Health Organisation, Europe (2004a) *Palliative Care: The Solid Facts*. Copenhagen: WHO.

World Health Organisation (2004b) *A Community Health Approach to Palliative Care for HIV and Cancer*. Geneva: WHO.

World Health Organisation, Europe (2004c) *Better Palliative Care for Older People*. Copenhagen: WHO.

World Health Organisation and International Union Against Cancer (UICC) (2002) *National Cancer Control Programmes: Policies and Managerial Guidelines* (2nd edn). Geneva: WHO.

Wright M (2003) *Models of Hospice and Palliative Care in Resource Poor Countries: Issues and Opportunities*. Lancaster: International Observatory on End-of-Life Care.

Wright PM (2001) A critical pathway for interdisciplinary hospice care. *Amer J Hospice Pall Care* **18**(1): 31–4.

Zimring SD (2001) Multi-cultural issues in advance directives. *J Amer Directors Assoc* **2**: 241–5.

Zuckerman C, Wollner D (1999) End-of- life care and decision-making: How far we have come, how far we have to go. In Z Corless (ed) *The Hospice Heritage: Celebrating Our Future*. Birmingham, NY: Haworth Press.

50plushealth (2003) *Support and Opposition to Assisted Dying Bill HMG Worldwide* [Accessed 21 October 2004]. From http://www.50plushealth. co.uk/index.cfm?articleid=2448

# Index

to refuse treatment
  a construct of developed world  18
Robert Wood Johnson Foundation  8, 62
Romania
  care development in  74
  end-of-life care in  80
Royal College of Nursing  39

## S

sanctity of life  42
Saunders, Dame Cecily  3
Schiavo, Terri  21, 23
shortness of breath  47
slippery slope arguments  46
Soros Foundation Project on Death in
      America  62
Spain
  care development in  74
  end-of-life care in  81–82
spiritual care  61
staffing
  in end-of-life care  59–63
  requirements  51
State Children's Health Program Benefits
      Improvement Act (2000)  54
stents  40
studied neutrality  46
sub-Saharan Africa  78
substituted judgment  19, 23
SUPPORT  7, 57, 65
support and capacity
  questions to ask  26
Supreme Court  21
Switzerland
  and legalisation of patient-assisted
      suicide  83

## T

Tanzania  78
terminal care  11
Termination of Life on Request and
      Assistance with Suicide Act  82
Terri's Law  22
therapeutic futility  41
trespass  31

trials of therapy  41
Turkey
  care development in  75
  end-of-life care in  80

## U

Uganda  78
  care development in  75
UKCC Code of Professional Conduct  30
UK Nursing and Midwifery Council  30
UK Pain Society  10
United Nations Single Convention on
      Narcotic Drugs  4
USA
  funding of end-of-life care  53
  futility  32

## V

*Vacco* v *Quill*  20, 21
valid consent
  requirements for  18
voluntary euthanasia  82
vomiting  47

## W

Wales  56
*Washington* v *Glucksberg*  20
weakness  47
WHO
  advisory booklets  10
  benchmarking tools  10
  *Cancer Pain Relief*  4
  influence on global developments
      69–76
  *Pain Relief and Palliative Care*  5
  practice manuals  10
Winston-Jones, Luke  43
workshops
  for clinicians  62
Wyatt, Charlotte  42–43
*Wyatt* v *Portsmouth NHS Trust*  43

## Z

Zimbabwe  78